Another Perfect Christmas:
The Perfect Gift

Helen Isolde Thomas

Believe

CONTENTS

Introductions

INTRODUCTION

Twenty years ago, I wrote and produced a small, hand-bound book, *How to Have a Perfect Christmas*. I started writing it on the day after Christmas, 1994, out of frustration. My inspiration came from a single negative comment stemming from a well-meant effort to make everything perfect. Here is what happened. I arrived at my aunt's house for the family Christmas dinner and celebration. The front door was ajar, so I opened it and stepped inside. The scene was indeed perfect. The house was elegantly decorated. Christmas music was playing, the table was set with fine china and crystal, and the delicious smells of a traditional roast beef with Yorkshire pudding dinner wafted from the kitchen, but there was no sign of my aunt. Instead of her warm smile and open arms waiting to give me a hug and share the joy of this special season, there was a strained voice shouting in annoyance from the kitchen.

"Next year," she screamed, "I'm going on a cruise for Christmas!"

Her message was clear. She was overwhelmed. Her comment left me bereft of holiday spirit, feeling unwelcome and slightly guilty for having been partly responsible for her frazzled state. The silver lining that shone through that cloudy gray family Christmas was that I began to think of the flip side of that kind of experience, of all the warm and wonderful things about the season; first and foremost, the Christ child, God's gift to mankind, and all the other related things that brought joy, the real things that could be appreciated without driving people to exhausted distraction. I thought about simple things, things we could do or not do to actually live the Christmas experience better and enjoy it more. It was a process, a project that helped me retrieve the holiday spirit.

I compiled close to 100 separate suggestions and was determined to share them. In the fall of 1995, I printed them at home on beige card stock and cut, hole-punched and bound the sheets into a small book, securing the pages with a length of red silk ribbon tied into a bow. It was more of a booklet than a book, these suggestions intended to help people appreciate the moments of the season and avoid the madness. Roughly one thousand copies sold in local gift shops and book stores. The next year, it was purchased by a major publishing house, expanded to include an introductory essay, appeared as the centerfold in their fall catalog. It was distributed nationally in time for the Christmas season, as *How to Have a Perfect Christmas: Practical and Inspirational Advice to Simplify Your Holiday Season* (Dutton 1996).

Everything seemed perfect in my writer's life. (spoiler alert: it wasn't.) I got a huge advance and flew to New York to have lunch with my agent. I toured the publisher's offices and met the artist who created the cover. I did book signings and radio drive-time, talk-show interviews by phone from home and in person. My local newspaper did a feature on me and dubbed me "the anti-Martha Stewart."

Then I, the queen of imperfection, came face to face with my own philosophy. The bottom fell out of my perfect life. A book club deal fell through. The proposed countertop display that would put my book right next to the register in bookstores across the county wasn't developed. And the list of radio stations wanting to talk to me dwindled to none. My agent explained that my editor had taken a job at a different publisher. My book had been "orphaned." The editor who chose it would no longer be there to promote it, and no one else would want to.

Like other holiday trappings, *How to Have a Perfect Christmas* was packed away, but apparently not forgotten. People still approach me at Christmastime to say that they bring the book out each year to look at it and enjoy it again and again. Last year, one family, unaware of the book's publication history, tracked me down through Facebook to see if I still had any copies of the original, hand-made version. I didn't, but their query inspired me to revive an idea that had been brewing in the back of my mind for some time—to republish it in another form. What if I looked at it again? What if I thought and wrote about some of those suggestions— where they had come from and what might they have meant to me at that time? What might they mean now, burnished with the glow of a perspective of twenty years of personal growth and cultural climate change?

I embarked on this effort unsure of how it might work. My suggestions may have been better as tiny bits of food-for-thought, appetizers rather than main course essays. Nevertheless, I forged ahead with this look back from the perspective of having moved on, and here is *Another Perfect Christmas: The Perfect Gift*. The suggestions are all the same and for the most part in the same order. The theme of the book has not changed. I still love Christmas and want everyone to make the most of it without making themselves crazy. The book is still not intended to be read in one sitting, but to be picked at and savored in small bites. The new subtitle has two meanings; one, that reading this book and having a good Christmas may be the perfect gift to yourself, your friends and your family; and two, that Christmas really is about the perfect gift from God, the gift of love. So how do you let go of perfection when we have all been taught to put our best foot forward? How do you make the most of a beautiful holiday without making yourself and others crazy? Read on.

Merry Perfect Christmas!

Helen Isolde Thomas, 2014

INTRODUCTION TO
HOW TO HAVE A PERFECT CHRISTMAS (Dutton, 1996)

Picture the perfect Christmas. Your elegant home is decorated with garlands of evergreen and holly. Your happy family is gathered around the glittering tree. Gaily wrapped gifts are piled up everywhere. The seasoned aroma of Christmas dinner streams from the kitchen, while outside, snow falls softly and the sounds of Christmas carols and sleigh bells fill the air. This is a fantasy.

Now, wake up, open your eyes, and welcome to reality. Your guests are late for dinner and the roast is charred beyond an arson investigator's recognition. Your family members are faint with hunger. The kids are fighting like trolls and you can't even threaten them with Santa because they opened their presents hours ago. Your cat takes a flying leap at a strand of tinsel and topples the tree. Grandma startles awake and spills her blackberry brandy on your carpet. Helpless, hopeless and exhausted, you teeter on the brink of insanity.

In spite of years of experience, and more than enough intelligence to know better, most of us still hold dear some version of the perfect Christmas deep in our hearts. It is a vision made up of childhood memories, high hopes and unrealistic expectations. But we always believe we can make it happen, if only we try hard enough. The fact is, we try too hard. We try to create and live a fantasy. We try to make it perfect, and instead Christmas becomes an annual crazy-making event. The harder we work at making Christmas perfect, the more likely we are to fall flat on our weary faces. Perfection is not possible. It is not a part of the human condition, nor is it even a definable goal. Real life is not choreographed, it is chaotic. Accepting that, we can learn to love it.

This book is my Christmas gift to you and to anyone who has ever struggled to make Christmas perfect. It is a collection of hard-learned lessons from many years of Christmas experience, some good advice from some good friends, and a little bit of whimsy. It grew from the realization that there are some few things in life that we can control but many more that we can't, some things that we can change, and lots more that won't be the least bit different in our lifetime or the next.

Some of these sayings are funny, some are serious; some offer advice that is easy to take, some speak to goals that are ideals. Taken together, they suggest that we look closely at what we are trying to do compared to what we are doing. You are a very important part of everyone's Merry Christmas. Relax and enjoy. The greatest gift we have to offer each other is ourselves: rested, cheerful, and ready to spend a perfectly happy holiday together.

Have a Perfectly Merry Christmas!

1

ACCEPT THE FACT THAT HOLIDAYS, LIKE PEOPLE, ARE NOT PERFECT.

I love Christmas. I really do, and I actually do believe that it has a true meaning, although you won't find me preaching sermons in these pages. Rather, I write about the day and season named for a Christian celebration that is wrapped up in ancient traditions and symbols, and that has also evolved to be a complex and multifaceted miracle of a time that gets many people thinking about giving and love. Yes, I lament the commercialism, but I don't spend too much time on that old soapbox either.

These pages have a simple and personal message – that getting carried away with trying to outdo yourself or your friends or neighbors or just making too much of an effort to make Christmas too perfect just might ruin it for you or your friends and family. Instead, there are thoughts and suggestions here to help you ponder what Christmas means to you and ideas to help you enjoy it.

Holidays are not perfect, never mind the glossy magazine covers that promise you can make them so. Those claims are false. They are made to sell magazines. If you strive for a perfect fantasy Christmas as flawless as the ones on all the magazine covers, heap that vision up with unrealistic expectations and then try to make it all happen, you are setting yourself up for disappointment and probably enough stress to ruin it for others. Fantasy and real life are two very different things. Real life is not staged with lights and backdrops nor is it airbrushed. Whatever you do or don't do, your Christmas will be unique and special because it is yours, and your traditions will be your very own.

God knows we humans are not perfect, no matter how hard we try or how good we look. Our many variables and vicissitudes create the rich texture of who and what we are, and that is what make us unique and special. Your Christmas will be perfect because you are a key part of it, not because you polished the silver to a satiny gleam or mastered the art of making gourmet butter cookies, but because it is infused with your being, your love, and your presence. Perfection is found and cherished in the times you spend together—times full of love, caring and laughter, times when you are not feeling stressed—perfect times.

2

REMEMBER, HAPPINESS IS WANTING WHAT YOU HAVE, NOT HAVING WHAT YOU WANT.

What the Charles Dickens does that mean? I'm not sure it even makes sense, and there is something rather smug about this reminder. Wanting something, by definition, seems to preclude the possibility that you already have it. Right? Isn't there something rather circular about this old adage? How can you want what you have when you already have it?

Maybe the circle takes us right back to the question of what we really want and the question of whether that is what will make us happy. Who wants a roof over their head? A family? A car? A job? A friend? Peace in their home? Peace in their homeland? Food? Healthcare? Freedom? Oh, you aren't currently wanting those, because you already have them? Of course, we'd be unhappy if we didn't have those things. We are reminded of that at this time of year by the endless appeals to support the hungry, the homeless or the just generally needy. They have good reason to be unhappy, but here's the funny thing, apparently so do we. According to the Happy Planet Index, the unhappiest countries in the world include the United States, along with much of sub-Saharan Africa, Mongolia and Afghanistan. See http://www.happyplanetindex.org/data/. The happiest country in the world is Costa Rica, one of the poorest.

Perhaps the measures used in that index (experienced well-being, life expectancy and ecological footprint) aren't the ones you would choose to measure your happiness, but how to achieve it is an age-old question. Aristotle weighed in on it, and the number of books you can buy to support your search for it is huge. Maybe it really is something as simple as wanting or recognizing what you have and being happy with that. The glass is half full or half empty.

I'm going with half full. I'm happy with that.

3

CHECK THE BATTERIES ON YOUR CAMERA AND BUY LOTS OF FILM.

An entire generation would be baffled by a box of film, no less at the thought of loading it into a camera, rewinding it and taking it or sending it out to be developed. I mean physically carrying it to a store or sending it through the mail, then getting back prints and negatives that you actually hold in your hand, put in scrapbooks or file. There is lots of good news and bad news here.

The good news: just think of all the paper and processing resources that have been saved! I would be embarrassed to admit how many photo albums I have collecting dust on the shelves. They will, I suspect, become a cursed legacy to my daughter and her descendants until one of them either digitizes or tosses them. More good news: In addition to sharing images online, we now also have the option to plaster them on coffee cups, calendars, or fabrics—images that we have been able to digitally perfect on our computers. Wow!

The battery thing, well, that problem has pretty much gone away. The largest percentage of point-and-shoot cameras, and of course tablets and cell phones that take what I call *phonetographs*, operate as rechargeable devices—good news for the electric companies. As for those things that still require batteries, well, that may be the bad news. Sustainable, efficient storage of power hasn't quite been mastered, and disposal of dead batteries remains a challenge. Let's check back in another twenty years on that one. I suspect it may be a whole different story.

For now, let's revise this suggestion to "Make sure you have an extra memory card, or that you have uploaded your images and that everything is fully charged."

4

CONTEMPLATE THE UNIQUE SYMMETRY OF A SINGLE SNOWFLAKE.

From the time I was a little girl, I have participated in an annual ritual, around Christmas, at which I am not very good. It is the cutting out of paper snowflakes that always disappoint me because they look so flat, so folded, and far too substantial to replicate the fluff that falls from the sky and creates an enchanted landscape. While living in England during my husband's sabbatical year, I made them because I had no decorations for my Christmas tree. At that time, the milk truck actually delivered fresh milk to our door every day, and each glass bottle was sealed with a foil cap. I washed the caps and cut them into little silver snowflakes and hung them on the tree with tiny bits of yarn from my knitting basket, along with colorful foil-wrapped candies. They were lovely, but still nothing like real snowflakes.

The first time I saw an actual photograph of a single snowflake was in *The Hidden Messages in Water*, by Masaru Emoto. That was the real stuff of enchantment. I could actually stare at detailed images of these tiny, fragile building blocks that could amass into mounds that would stop traffic. The pictures show crystalline structures that are ephemeral, fragile, and startlingly beautiful in their design and translucence. The magic is there, just like it is in the gentle flakes outside your window that are so impossible to replicate. Seeing such perfect symmetry on such an unimaginable and humanly impossible scale is humbling. There are some things we just can't do and shouldn't even try. Contemplating the miracle of a single snowflake puts compiling a tray of hors d'oeuvres into a whole new perspective. It's really not such a big deal after all.

5

PLAN THE CHRISTMAS MENU KNOWING THAT THE COOK DESERVES A HOLIDAY TOO.

We love to think of traditions at Christmas that hark back to a romanticized Europe of yesteryear—a delicious and extravagant menu, the elaborate table settings and decorations, the gracious behaviors of host and guests. Guess what? Yours is not a Victorian household complete with downstairs staff to prepare for the festivities that you will so graciously host. Oh no, chances are you are planning on your lunch hour, cleaning all weekend, and cooking and baking after the kids have gone to bed, sacrificing your own sleep and sanity in the process. Those amazing cookie trays pictured on the cover of magazines were not made by working moms like you. They were made by professional chefs in corporate kitchens, by people who do those things for a living while you are hard at work running the medical, judicial or financial systems that support their efforts and rearing your children as well.

Increasingly, I see online pictures comparing real life failed results to professional recipe photos. We may know our *croquembouche* won't stack up properly, but for some reason, we get particularly vulnerable to attempting more than we likely can do at Christmastime. It's as if the holiday compromises our understanding of what we are actually capable of accomplishing, as if we think that taking on such a grandiose challenge shows we care. We need to care enough for our guests to want to give them our time in person, not in the kitchen, and we need to care for ourselves too. If you can try that 26-ingredient, two-day long gourmet recipe without stressing yourself, and laugh when the whole thing collapses, go ahead and do it. If not, do something sensible like buying a cake at the bakery or choosing a good brownie mix and serving it with peppermint ice cream and chocolate syrup so everyone can build their own sundae. It will be fun for all, including the cook.

6

APPRECIATE THE FACT THAT THE COLD OUTSIDE MAKES
YOU FEEL WARM INSIDE.

This was easier to say when the entire country wasn't caught up
and whirled around in a polar vortex. Now it sounds sort of
cutesy, sort of Currier and Ives Christmas card scene where the
people sitting in the horse-drawn sleigh look ever so comfortable.
Just imagine how cold that must have been. We don't even open
our car windows in winter. And they didn't even have Polartec.
Maybe the cold was picturesque then and snowflakes fell straight
down and there was no wind in winter and everybody was
perfectly happy in their wool coats and leather boots which must
have leaked horribly. That's how the pictures on our Christmas
cards look.

I hate the cold. I have always hated the cold and I can't honestly
say if I hate it more at twenty degrees Fahrenheit than at fifteen,
although the latter temperature if sustained over a few days is far
more likely to freeze my water pipes than the former, and this
does impact my attitude. So many of us have been traumatized by
extreme weather in recent years, it has become tedious to

complain about it and sounds foolhardy to suggest it can make you feel warm.

I'm not sure now exactly what I meant when I wrote this. Did I mean that sitting by the fire and looking out at the foul weather elicits the warm fuzzy feeling that we expect to have at Christmas? The one and only cure I have ever found for feeling cold in the house in winter is to go outside. I simply bundle up in additional layers and all the outerwear I can manage to fit over what I'm wearing, and venture outside. It feels really warm when I come back in. So the "inside" here is not the ET heart glow in my chest while sitting by the fireside, but rather the temperature inside the house that feels wonderful after I have been outside even for just a short time. In addition, any of us fortunate enough to have a home to come into out of the cold can experience an inner warmth just from an attitude of gratitude.

7

"SOME ASSEMBLY REQUIRED" DOES NOT MEAN YOU CAN PUT IT TOGETHER ON CHRISTMAS EVE.

The "some assembly" ritual is often carried out on Christmas Eve, after the kids have been sent to bed, when parents' nerves and energy have already been strained to the breaking point. Directions are likely not written on paper, but rather are only available at www\http:goodluckfindingthese.net. If they do appear on a small, folded piece of paper, they are probably written in at least seven languages side by side, in a print size that only a flea could read. More likely, they are simply a series of numbered pictures or diagrams divided into a number of steps. The pictures have very little resemblance to the parts that come out of the box, and only a fool would expect that Tab A will fit into Slot B as the picture indicates it should. Nowhere does it offer any explanation of what to do when things don't match, nor is there ever any contact information for assistance.

The good news is that these are the kind of trying times that we later look back on and find that they provoke hilarious laughter. There are several things you can do, if you have the misfortune of finding yourself facing an unassembled gift on Christmas Eve. First, recognize immediately that putting this item together is not as important as maintaining your sanity or keeping your marriage intact. Second, try to imagine that at some point in the future this will make you laugh. Third, pack it up and go to bed, knowing that you need your sleep more than the child needs to open this assembled. Forth, resort to the duct tape solution. Fifth, leave it unassembled and use it as a teaching tool for your child. Chances are, they may be able to put it together, anyway.

8

LISTEN WELL TO SOMEONE WHO IS FEELING DISAPPOINTED.

I couldn't have said this twenty years ago, but I have lots of really cool Facebook friends. Recently, my friend Lou posted a quote from iBelieve.com via Baisden Live. "Everyone you meet is fighting a battle you know nothing about. Be kind. Always."

This lesson has come to us from all the great teachers of wisdom throughout the ages in one form or another. What I was thinking when I originally wrote this was actually twofold. First, be aware that each of us is likely fighting some silent battle whether it is obvious or not, and, second, the best gift you can give anyone is to listen well, if they want to talk.

Listening well is not a passive activity. Listening well involves a fair amount of effort. It means not just being open to hear what another person says, but seeking what they want to say. For years, I have been paying very close attention to how people respond to the casual "How are you?" question. If I get anything less than an enthusiastically positive, "Great, good, really good" I take that as a conversation opening clue to finding out how that person really is. Anyone who responds, "OK" will hear me follow up with, "Just OK?"

There are any number of reasons why people may be feeling disappointed at any time of year. It could be as simple as having missed one of the last items on sale at the "doorbuster" price, or, it could be someone's leave was canceled, or they've lost a loved one, or some other emotional or physical pain is draining them of the possibility of fully experiencing the joy of the season. What matters is that we, as caring human beings, don't let our own busyness or disappointment interfere with our awareness of, or compassion for others.

9

REMEMBER, YOU GET ANOTHER CHANCE NEXT YEAR.

Okay, so you didn't finish the afghan you were going to give to your future daughter-in-law and opted instead for a gift card. Don't beat yourself up, never mind that nagging unfinished afghan in your knitting basket and your fears that she will doubt that you care enough to come up with something personal. This year's Christmas gift is not going to define your relationship forever with anyone. It may not even be remembered. I love gifts, but have a bad memory, and so every year, my family gets a kick out of the Gift Question Game. It goes something like this:

"What did I give you last year that was small and flat?"

I make probable guesses, "A gift card? A book?" But, I'm almost always stumped to remember a year later. Maybe they just give me bad clues, or forgettable gifts, I don't know, but we do have a great deal of fun.

Another annual ritual occurs after Christmas when I do a little informal assessment of how I did preparing for the holiday. I resolve to apply some quality improvement for next year. I go out

17

and snag that $7-a-roll paper at 75% off and stash a few choice sale items that seem like they will be the perfect gift for someone next year. Then all those good intentions fall prey to the passage of time and my bad memory over the following months, and by fall, I'm lucky if I can even find the stuff I bought or if anything seems even remotely appropriate as a gift for anyone I ever met.

We all know that Christmas comes every year. It even comes on the same day every year. There are certainly plenty of reminders that it is getting closer, starting long before what any reasonable person would call the Christmas Season. So every year when it comes up (and it does keep coming back), we have a chance to decide whether it makes sense to try to reach that unreachable and unrealistic state of perfection in gift giving, decorating or whatever.

Maybe a knitting project is a great idea, but for next year, not this. Just think of how pleasant it would be to have the luxury of time to knit it. And maybe you could spend some time with the prospective gift recipient shopping for a color of yarn or pattern they would love to have, or maybe knitting it together. You could put a note in a card pledging to do this. You don't have to make yourself crazy this year. There is always next year.

10

COMMUNICATE.

A few decades back, communication was a buzzword, touted as the be-all and end-all of successful personal and corporate relationships. Dozens of how-to books on myriads of methods were written about effective communication. Thousands of corporate PowerPoint presentations addressed its sensitivities, power and processes. And then came the electronic revolution when communication became instantaneous in text, sound and moving images for everyone, almost no matter where you were in this country except for a few scattered places like New York's Adirondack Park or maybe some places in Wyoming. We have almost come full circle now, with a movement toward "slow communication," that which does not rely on any source of artificially generated power. And barring all those other instruments of potential electronic contact, we may once again focus on person to person communication.

The word *communicate* stems from *com* the same root word as *commune,* and it means "to share," in this case to share understanding. If you think of your communications as efforts to share understanding, you might get a little closer to saying exactly what you mean and to being understood. Sharing involves more than one person. It's a two-way process. It's not a tweet, an email, or an annual, multiple-copy Christmas letter. Those may convey information, but they are not really communicating. Real communication is different; it's person to person.

Try it (with my apologies to those who send annual Christmas letters—no offense intended). Just try it.

11

REMEMBER, HOLIDAY CHEER DOES NOT COME IN A BOTTLE.

Movies from the yesteryear of my youth, always showed the most handsome actors and beautiful actresses, all the brightest stars, tipping a glittering cocktail glass in just about every setting and scene possible, and television perpetuated the association of alcohol with glamour and good humor. But a number of high-profile figures, beginning with Betty Ford, as well as national publications and a series of films, including *The Days of Wine and Roses (1962), Who's Afraid of Virginia Woolf (1966), Under the Volcano (1984), Barfly* (1987), *Leaving Las Vegas (1995), Bad Santa (2003), and Flight* (2112) have attempted to tell alcohol's real story. In spite of these efforts, alcohol's glamorous image persists, and we continue to see and serve alcohol as an important part of holiday cheer. Images of beautiful people drinking alcohol in elegant settings that most of us may never visit, no less inhabit, prevail over what we know to be the dangers and downside. We may never be able to unglamorize alcohol, but when drinking or serving alcohol during the holiday season, remember that the good cheer of the season isn't in the bottle, regardless of the images conveyed in advertising and the specially labeled holiday bottles. This suggestion reminds us of the reality.

> An estimated 17 million Americans have an alcohol use disorder (AUD)—a medical term that includes both alcoholism and harmful drinking that does not reach the level of dependence, and each year in the United States, nearly 85,000 people die from alcohol-related causes, making it the third leading preventable cause of death in our country.
> National   Institute on Alcohol Abuse and Alcoholism
> http://www.niaaa.nih.gov/alcohol-health/overview-alcohol-consumption/alcohol-facts-and-statistics
> (Retrieved 7/15/14)

12

WHILE SHOPPING, PRETEND YOU ARE WALKING FOR EXERCISE.

I have a problem with this suggestion, maybe partly because I have a problem with walking for exercise. Two problems, actually. First, it hurts my knees, and second, it never really has felt like exercise except for the time I was hooked up to an EKG on a treadmill and required to fast-walk uphill to increase my heart rate to a level that even the cardiologist didn't recommend as good practice. Can you really pretend your shopping hike into the mall from your remote parking spot is exercise and good for you? This sounds somewhat like setting your clocks ahead so you won't be late. You can't really fool yourself, just like you can't really tickle yourself.

You can change your behavior or change your attitude. Here are some suggestions to change your shopping behavior:

- ❖ Shop early (as in early in the year or early expanded store hours)

- ❖ Take the bus. It will drop you where you want to go.

- ❖ Shop online.

- ❖ Let your fingers do the walking. (For those of you born after 1960, this means research in a published directory and shop by phone.)

Here are some suggestions to change your attitude:

- ❖ Ask yourself whether you really deserve that close-in parking spot more than the person who got it.

- ❖ Breathe deeply and stretch periodically.

- ❖ Get over it!

- ❖ Read this book.

13

THINK ABOUT SOMEONE WHO IS TRYING TO THINK OF
THE PERFECT GIFT FOR YOU.
DON'T EXPECT TO HAVE THE PERFECT GIFT FOR
EVERYONE. YOU WON'T, NOR WILL THEY.

These were two separate entries in the original version of this book, but now I find it difficult to separate them. Doesn't the thought of someone thinking of you just warm your heart? Do you really care if what they get you is perfect? Or, do you care about that person, and hope they don't stress too much about a gift? I hope it's the latter, if you are one of my friends reading this.

Sometimes when I am out shopping or traveling, or reading book reviews, I come upon something that strikes me as the absolutely perfect gift for someone. It's an exhilarating feeling when am so sure they will love it. But it is not something I can hope will happen all the time.

This shouldn't come as a surprise. Nobody has the perfect gift for everyone. Ever, unless they are only buying for a bunch of children of the same age all of whom want the same thing, and they happen to have the good fortune of finding a plentiful supply of that must-have toy of the year.

Some people are really hard to give gifts to, either because they seem to have everything, or because they are hard to please. You may never find the perfect gift for them. Of course, your heart is in the right place when you search for a gift for everyone you love, isn't it? There is no question of one-upmanship or pride or anything like that, is there? Surely not.

14

HAVE EXTRA C, D, AND 9 VOLT BATTERIES ON HAND.

What was I thinking? What about double and triple As? I guess this suggestion still holds true, although many of today's power-consuming presents come with chargers. Really people! A gift that doesn't work when you open it isn't really a good gift. Read the box. It will say whether the item needs batteries or not, and it will tell you what size it needs, although admittedly all of this may be written in microscopic-size Aramaic text. Open it if you have to and make sure it works. Charge it if it comes with a charger. What could be more disappointing than getting what you wanted but not getting it yet. "Oh, wow! Just what I wanted, thank you sooo much. I'll just plug it in now and watch it charge for the next six hours." I think you get the idea.

I have to admit that this is adding a little bit to the stuff you have to do in preparation for Christmas, but you will already have saved so much time following the other suggestions in this book, that you will have plenty of time to take this precaution.

And it will be so much better for the recipient of your gift to have a working item. Then, instead of spending the next six hours waiting for something to charge, they can spend the next six hours trying to figure out how it works.

15

ASSESS YOUR EXPECTATIONS OF YOURSELF AND OTHERS, THEN LOWER THEM.

Expectations. What are they? They are stories we tell ourselves and believe or assume to be true about how things will or ought to be. They are the stories that reflect the images of our hopes. Some are based on experience, like we expect the sun to rise and the moon to impact the tides at regular intervals. Some are based on our preferences, like I expect people to hold doors open for each other and to respect their elders and to not kill each other. Oh dear, that doesn't always happen, does it? That, I think, is where we get into trouble with expectations. They all pretty much come down to how we think everything and everybody ought to be. Well, I guess we all know by now, that just isn't the way things work, and high expectations can lead to high levels of disappointment.

Sam Walton would, no doubt, debate me on this one. He has been quoted as saying that "High expectations are the key to everything." I expect his words are held up in MBA programs and motivational seminars on a routine basis, so if building a retail empire and unimaginable personal wealth at whatever cost to everyone else is your goal, then close this book right now and go read something else.

High expectations of yourself and others around the Christmas holiday can be extremely dangerous. The overstressed clerk just may not be as courteous as you expect, and the Christmas dinner you planned so carefully just may not be as spectacularly received as you expected. There are likely good reasons for these circumstances. Be flexible. Don't let your expectations become the basis of your stress. Hope for the best, but, don't stand in judgment of everything that doesn't measure up to your expectations. You can make yourself and everybody else miserable if you do.

16

LIVE EVERY MOMENT AND CHERISH IT.

Do you live in the past? The future? Do you have regrets? I've been guilty of all the above, suffering remorse over things I did or didn't do at one point or trying to recapture what was or what might have been, and then on other days worrying about or planning so much that I was barely present in the present.

What if you got to the end, old and tired, or perhaps suffering from a painful and lingering disease, and someone told you that you could have another twenty-four hours in good health? Yes, that is not possible, but the point is, what would you do with that time? How would it feel? Wouldn't you really cherish every moment you had? If you can capture that perspective, you can change right now. What if those twenty-four hours were at Christmas? We only have to go as far as Charles Dickens's Scrooge to see how that might work.

I think I'll change this suggestion to "Read *A Christmas Carol*."

> Best and happiest of all, the time before him was his own, to make amends in! 'I will live in the Past, the Present, and the Future!' Scrooge repeated, as he scrambled out of bed. 'The Spirits of all Three shall strive within me. Oh Jacob Marley! Heaven, and the Christmas Time be praised for this. I say it on my knees, old Jacob, on my knees!'

> After that, "it was always said of him, that he knew how to keep Christmas well, if any man alive possessed the knowledge. May that be truly said of us, and all of us!

> *A Christmas Carol,* Stave 5, *The End of It*,
> by Charles Dickens

17

UNDERSTAND THAT ONLY YOU CAN MAKE YOURSELF LESS BUSY.

Only you can control the busyness of your life, although it may require a basic shift in your pursuit of what you think you want out of life. For my secular readers, Carl Honore's *In Praise of Slowness* (HarperOne, 2005) traces the history of our increasingly breathless relationship with time and tackles the consequences of living in this accelerated culture of our own creation. Arianna Huffington's book *Thrive* (Harmony, 2014) tells how she came to realize that her definition of success and the life she was pursuing needed to change. A world-famous, successful career woman, she collapsed from exhaustion, breaking her cheekbone and gashing her head as she fell. Her book proposes a different definition for success, one that includes well being. In *Well Being: The Five Essential Elements* (Gallup,2010), Tom Rath and Jim Harter point out that we sometimes focus on one element of our lives (career, social, money, health, or community) expecting that one to bring happiness when all are interdependent.

But for Christians, the Bible story of the birth of Jesus is all that's necessary to read, in order to remember where to find balance. There is the centering point for life, the yardstick against which all activities can be measured. How do the things that you are doing this Christmas actually relate to this miracle or incorporate its significance? This humble, simple, slow-paced story tells it all. An unimaginable gift from God is delivered to a woman who arrived by donkey at a stable—not the stuff of your average glossy cover.

18

SPEND AN EVENING RECALLING YOUR FAVORITE HOLIDAY MEMORIES.

One Christmas, my daughter and I volunteered to help hand out gifts to needy children on Christmas morning. I don't remember what year that was, or what civic or charitable organizations had set up a mall Santa and huge pile of gifts in the lobby of a closed bank. I do remember what a unique and wonderful feeling it was to see so many children approach with hesitation and grasp to their chests what might have been the only wrapped present they would get that year. And I remember that we left there filled with joy for having had the opportunity to volunteer our time to help staff this event.

What I remember most about my childhood family Christmases are the traditions we observed every year, starting with the Germanic custom of Christmas Eve festivities. First we got dressed up and went to church together as a family. We sang Christmas hymns, and often my father would perform a solo version of *O, Holy Night* or *Lo, How a Rose Ere Blooming*. We shared the candle flame to the soft strains of *Silent Night*. At home, we gathered around the Christmas tree, while our father read again the story of the birth of Jesus from the *Book of Luke,* and our mother prepared snacks. I would like to say we listened patiently, but we knew that soon after the reading was done, we would open our presents. We must have been bursting with anticipation, and yet, I remember very few of the presents I received, but I can still see the family gathering in my mind's eye as clearly as if it happened yesterday, and I always know what was the greatest gift of all.

What memories do you have or are you creating? Sit with the ones you love and ask them about their holiday memories; you may rethink what you want to do in the future. How will this year look next year? How would you like it to be remembered?

19

BE SPIRITUAL.

Church attendance soars at Christmas and at Easter. Is that when people feel spiritual? Is that the only time? Don't get me wrong. The last thing I would want to do is chase these people away from church by questioning their motives. I'm not suggesting that people should feel bad about showing up on those Sundays. Those who are there regularly love to hear the swell of voices in the hymns sung. They love to see the smiling faces and to make connections with people they see only rarely or in different contexts. They love to see that the visitors share the joy of these occasions. They love to welcome them and share God's peace with them.

There really is no "us and them" among the occasional and regular churchgoers. They are all the same. They have the same the same experiences, the same doubts, the same health and family problems, and even sometimes the same faith. If you are one of those who attends church regularly, remember that and welcome those who are only able to drop in sporadically. If you are one of those who drops in, know that you are welcome. Know that you are welcome in God's house at those times or any other. If the church you visit doesn't make you feel welcome, find one that does.

What could be better than to have the church packed full of people on Christmas Eve while the candles are lit to the soft strains of "Silent Night"? That's being spiritual.

20

ALLOW YOURSELF TO GRIEVE FOR PEOPLE WHO ARE NO LONGER HERE.

After a more than twenty-year battle with cancer, my father, Gus, died the day before Christmas Eve in December 2001. It was a tragic year all around. That Christmas was a dark time, as we struggled to manage both our national (9/11) and personal grief along with questions about when to schedule funeral services during the holidays. We retreated into grief that long, cold winter and were reminded again and again of our loss in following years' Christmases. The joy of Christmas is hard to deny or ignore, but ours has been touched with that memory ever since. Since then, I have always tried to recognize the fact that for many, the holidays might not be the most joyful time.

There is an odd feeling of disconnection when a loved one dies and the rest of the world continues on as if nothing was different. In fact, we all have to continue on as soon as we can or must. There are jobs to attend to, meals to be prepared and consumed, children to care for, and holidays to observe. But there is also a need to grieve.

Remember Ecclesiastes 3:1:

> To everything there is a season, and a time to every purpose under the heaven: A time to be born, and a time to die;...A time to weep, and a time to laugh; a time to mourn, and a time to dance.

I wept, and I mourned my father's passing, and I am reminded of him at that time each year, just as we all remember our communal loss on September 11th. I still miss him, but I secretly console myself with the thought that he wanted to get home in time for the Jesus' birthday party in 2001, and I imagine him sharing the great joy in Heaven every year. Though theologically suspect, the thought helps me to smile and feel joyful in time for Christmas.

21

CUT YOUR SOCIAL CALENDAR IN HALF.

What does your December date book or calendar look like? What would it look like if you eliminated half of what was there? Is every weekend booked? Week nights? Lunches? When did you think you were going to do everything else you expected to do for Christmas?

Cutting social commitments might be the easiest way to free up some time and to free yourself from stress around the holidays. The family Christmas Eve service and celebrations and the Christmas Day dinner are probably the most important things you ought to do to. Consider your family events the essential social activities for the month, and beyond that any charity or community outreach efforts you can fit in. There may be a mandatory office Christmas party that is, unfortunately unavoidable. If there are too many of those kinds of commitments in your life, then go ahead and take your family on a vacation during December, so you have a good excuse to avoid them. If you must attend social commitments that devour your time and leave you tired, plan to leave them early. Even pared down to these essentials, your December datebook will look busy. There just isn't a lot of time. This year, Christmas Day, the 25th, is on a Thursday, which means there are exactly three weekends in December before the holiday in which you are free to do all your shopping, wrapping, card writing, baking, cooking, decorating, and whatever else you think you have to do in addition to social activities.

Why would you give up this precious time for, say, a cocktail party? Don't get me wrong. Parties can be fun, and there are people it's nice to see, although most parties don't allow for much quality connecting time. If you really care to see the people who invite you, why not plan a get together during that vast, dark, cold winter span of time between Christmas and Easter? Have a Superbowl party, a Valentine or a Mardi Gras party. Fat Tuesday seems like a wonderful time to indulge. The key here is to consider carefully and realistically what you can and what you really want to do, and to be proactive about not stretching yourself to the breaking point. Learn to say "No" graciously, to save yourself, and your sanity. Your friends may actually be happy to be relieved of a social obligation as well.

22

BURN CANDLES.

Candles are tiny fires that warm the heart. They are replete with a rich mix of ceremony, spirituality, symbolism, mystery, history and memories. They imply stillness in their fragile vulnerability to the slightest breeze, but they can burn. They are made of humble stuff, but they enhance the highest ceremonies of all sorts. They have the power to overcome darkness. They shed the softest light with the gentlest of glows and have done so for thousands of years. Around Christmas, candles bring anticipation with the weekly lighting of the Advent wreath and the moving Christmas Eve candlelight service.

I spent one Christmas Eve in the tiny village of Moutathal, Switzerland. It is hard to convey the darkness of a deep mountain valley on a winter night. The patch of sky between the huge black mountains was a clear deep blue-black, and a thin, pale moon glowed in it. I followed a narrow path up the side of the hill to the tiny Baroque church. Most of the villagers were there, reverently quiet. Outside the church, candles burned in red glass jars set on the stones in the tiny cemetery. Inside, the candlelight service was in Swiss German, but I didn't need to understand the words. The lighting of the candles and the feeling in the church were the same whether we were singing Silent Night or *Stille Nacht*. Later, at the house I was visiting, candles were lit on the Christmas tree - real candles—a beautiful custom, a close, personal silent night.

There is no light that symbolizes Christmas more than that of a candle, even a single small candle. Light comes in the darkness of the world. Humble. Powerful. Mysterious. Burn candles.

23

SEE THE ANGELS AMONG US.

In one of the most monumental incidents of bad timing in my life, I had the idea to write a book about angels. I envisioned a children's book and even got an artist friend of mine to do some preliminary sketches. I thought of an adult book with other angels, the powerful frightening Biblical angels who always seemed to scare people, and the ornate angels in Victorian art, the cherubic baby *putti* of the Renaissance. Wow! There were angels everywhere, and I wanted to write about them. But no one seemed to be interested, so I abandoned the idea. About ten years later, angel books started showing up everywhere. And angels appeared on everything from coffee mugs to wrapping paper, date books and carry bags, and I chided myself with a good dose of regret for not persisting with my planned texts, and for listening to the naysayers.

These popularized decorative angels are not the ones I'm suggesting we seek to see, but rather the real ones, the obvious ones like Mother Theresa, the hospice and rescue workers of the world, the heroic soldiers, public safety officers and teachers who put themselves in harm's way to protect others. But I also think there are angels among us, interacting, bringing us messages, standing on our shoulders or right behind us, guiding us to do the right thing, a Godly manifestation of conscience and more. Hebrews 13:2 says, "Forget not to show love unto strangers: for thereby some have entertained angels unawares."

The thought that there might just be something that special about any stranger I encounter is enough to make me think twice about how I treat them. What would the world be like if each of us saw the other as potentially an angel?

24

CUT YOUR GIFT LIST IN HALF.

Let's face it. A gift that isn't from the heart isn't really a gift. It's an exchange, a transaction, kind of like a credit to your conscience account, one that eases some sense of obligation. Chances are, you try to find the best gift at the lowest price to satisfy that obligation. Is that really a gift? Does that process warm the cockles of your heart in any way, or does it just provide a sense of relief for having accomplished the task and a certain level of satisfaction? Do you really think the recipient feels the love?

Admittedly, some people really are obligated to buy for a bunch of people. (Office managers are particularly adept at finding something that nobody wants, but everyone is required to be grateful for.) If you are in that position, you have my sympathy. All I can think to suggest is to get some sort of input from the group. If you are not one of those people, then stop this nonsense. People who lose their jobs stop, and nobody thinks twice about the economic justification for that. Why don't we all recognize the issue of sincerity as justification? All you would really have to tell anyone is that you are cutting back your gift list for a number of personal reasons (not that you really don't want another fruitcake). Why let Christmas devolve to an exchange of tokens for the sake of self gratification?

All you have to do is drive around a bit and look at the exponential growth of storage units to realize that most of us have way more stuff than we need. As I write this, four of my neighbors are setting up a massive garage sale, which seems to be an annual ritual that attempts to redistribute stuff people don't need in exchange for space and some amount of cash. My family already gets a kick out of imitating my frequently repeated and completely frustrated chant that comes out when I can't find something. "Too much stuff," is what I wail. "Too much stuff." And, they know not to give me anything that isn't consumable. Who needs it?

25

IF ONE STORE IS OUT OF SOMETHING, RESOLVE NOT TO LOOK FOR IT ELSEWHERE.

Who has ever done this? Show of hands. Come on, nobody's looking, and if they are, they'll just wonder what you're doing, maybe just think you are stretching.

I've done it. Remember Cabbage Patch Kids? I'm ashamed to say I went to every single store in town with a greedy gleam in my eye. I wanted one for my daughter, who desperately wanted one, and I wasn't going to leave out any possible chance of finding one. I probably even asked at the hardware store. Never mind the news reports or the sold out signs on the shelves. I just knew that if I kept trying, that somehow, by the Grace of God, I would hit a store that just got a shipment or stumble upon someone returning one. I would be there to get it. I would score the unavailable doll, phony birth certificate from the Babyland General Hospital and all.

That was a long time ago, and I was young and foolish and trying to be Supermom. Needless to say, I wore myself out, could have been spending time with my daughter instead, and more than likely was a bit abrupt if not downright rude to at least one store clerk or other customer. I did not get the doll. I spent long hours on many nights making a stocking doll imitation instead. I probably should have done that in the first place.

Fad gifts are mass produced now and can often be ordered online even before they are produced, but if you run across something you really think you need to buy and it falls into this kind of scarcity, don't knock yourself out. Spend your time with the person you were hoping to buy it for instead. Postpone the purchase and explain your decision. The item will be available later and both the shopper and the recipient will be better off for waiting.

26

BAKE COOKIES ONLY AS LONG AS YOU ENJOY THE PROCESS.

My house used to be known among friends, family and neighbors as the go-to place for Christmas cookies. Here, at the cookie queen's house, you could find the most delicate butter cookies; jam strips, *langues de chat*, Mexican wedding cakes, lightly almond-flavored and beautifully frosted and decorated cut outs, subtle orange macaroons with bittersweet chocolate drizzle, spicy fresh ginger bars and layered delicacies of shortbread, caramel and dark chocolate. I loved the process, and everyone loved the cookies. I started early in the holiday season and early every morning to make these confections. I carefully plotted out which ones would freeze well and made those first. Then I made and stored the ones that stayed fresh the longest in tightly lidded tins, finally finishing in the last week before Christmas with those with butter cream frosting that needed to be kept very fresh in the refrigerator. Everyone was welcome to join in the process, and kid-decorated cookies were considered as special as any of the more artistic endeavors. The point was we had fun. By Christmas, there were stacks and stacks of tins of cookies stored in strategically placed areas of the house, climatically appropriate to their needs. Whenever we entertained, or whenever anyone stopped in, we would haul out the tins and prepare plates or to-go bags with a grand variety of these bite sized bits of pure love.

I eventually did give up my former level of production, even though I loved it because my family of helpers moved away, and I ended up making and eating entirely too many of the cookies myself. It became a chore, and so eventually cookie production levels bottomed out at next to nothing in my house. Then I figured out that there are easier ways to always have a cookie tray ready at Christmas. There are lots of bakeries around that do a great job with cookies. And while the fanciest ones are pretty expensive, there are ways to get around that. You can spread a delicious homemade frosting on simple tinned cookies, or buy a few of the really fancy ones and put them on a tray with boxed, ready to bake, or the easiest-cookie-recipes-in-the-world kind with a few foil-wrapped candies for a festive-looking plate.

ONE OF THE EASIEST COOKIE RECIPES IN THE WORLD (WHICH IS ALSO GLUTEN FREE)

PEANUT BUTTER KISSES WITHOUT ALL THOSE MESSY DRY INGREDIENTS

1 c peanut butter
1 c sugar
1 egg
Mix and drop onto parchment-covered cookie sheets.
Bake at 350 for about 8 minutes.
Put chocolate kisses on just before they are done or drizzle them with melted chocolate when they come out.

27

DON'T GIVE ANYONE FRUITCAKE UNLESS YOU KNOW THEY LOVE IT.

Fruitcake of some sort or other has apparently been around for thousands of years. It seems the Romans made something like it, and variations in how it is made can be found around the world, partly because the British fell in love with it a few hundred years ago and they transplanted it along with other bits of their culture throughout their vast empire. In this country, it ranges from a convenient mail order or mall stand choice for the person who has everything, to a joke (thanks to late night talk show hosts), or a game. Some families trade the same fruitcake back and forth each year, and the Colorado town of Manitou Springs has an annual fruitcake toss if you want to get in on the fun. In whatever form, it has become baked into our fantasized Christmas traditions.

For me, though I caution against it, fruitcake brings warm and loving memories to mind, thoughts of some of the most wonderful neighbors I ever had. May and Emory Howard were two of the most amazing, God-fearing, friendly, and all-around delightful people one might ever dream could live next door. They looked a little like Mr. and Mrs. Appledoll. They were always smiling radiantly, in spite of evidence that they had as many and as difficult life challenges as anyone else, if not more.

My first Christmas in California and away from family, I was missing more than the snow back east. May not only gifted us with a box of her tiny, delicious fruitcake gems, but she agreed to show me how to make them. What I remember besides how good they were, is the warmth, friendship and fun we had making them.

I know that it is hard to believe how good they are, unless you try these, and it's an expensive and time consuming experiment, but trust me, they are really good, and yes, they can be made ahead. Probably the most important ingredient would be a good friend or neighbor to make them with. I can give you the recipe, but you will have to find your own friend. May you make as delicious tidbits and as lovely and long-lived memories as we did.

MAY HOWARD'S FRUITCAKE GEMS RECIPE

2 ½ c. candied cherries

1 c. chunk candied pineapple

1 c. diced mixed peels

1 c. quartered pitted dates

1 c. California Port

1 ½ c. pecan halves

2 eggs

¾ c. brown sugar

1 tsp. vanilla

½ tsp. almond extract

2 tbs. butter

¾ c. flour

½ tsp. salt

½ tsp. baking powder

Prepare fruits and peels.

(May has left this direction a little vague, but I think she means to measure them out.)

Add Port and mix well.

Cover and let stand 24 hours, turning several times.

Add nuts when ready to mix batter.

Beat eggs until thick and foamy. Beat in brown sugar and flavoring, then butter.

Resift flour with salt and baking powder. Add egg mixture and stir to blend. Add fruit mixture and mix well. Spoon into greased, floured (or papered) mini muffin pans and bake with a pan of water in the bottom of the oven, for 30 minutes or until they test done.

They will not be very cake-like, but more like the dried fruit/nut bars you can buy now, only homemade with a touch of love.

28

RESOLVE TO SET TIME ASIDE FOR YOURSELF.

Hi, I'm Helen, and I'm a TV-holic. Well, it's not quite that bad, but I must confess that I do watch TV. I even sometimes watch stupid TV. But here's the thing. I allow myself to watch TV in order to relax and let my brain rest. In a recent phone conversation, I mentioned that to someone. The person I was talking to said, "Yes, that can be a trap," and I realized immediately that I saw it as something quite different.

I rise very early every day. I work all day. I can't say that I don't sit down, because some of my work, writing, requires that I do so. I also garden, run around town doing errands, tend to three cats and a fish, paint (as in walls, rooms and the garage) clean, mow the lawn, wash my car and do any number of other things until about 5:30 or 6 at night when I have a light supper and clean up. So I've been active for about 13 hours. Then I watch TV. At the same time, I knit, or check social media, play an online word game with my sister, or look through a catalog or a magazine and then go to bed early. My TV time is my time for myself. It is essential for my mental health. I don't feel the least bit guilty about it.

I understand that not everybody can construct a schedule just the way they want it. I hope and pray that they are able to carve-out mini-moments just for themselves. Even the most selfless person needs to take care of him/her self, if they want to continue caring for others. And if TV is your guilty pleasure, go for it.

29

SEEK REST.

For those of you who are too busy to rest, here is something to add to your busy schedule: rest. Yes, rest. Schedule it in along with all the other important things you have to do. It's important.

A day of rest is built into most religious traditions, and valiant battles were fought by organized labor to achieve the 40-hour work week so people could rest. Physicians and athletes understand the rejuvenating significance of rest. Even horse trainers argue that the third leg of the Triple Crown disadvantages the winner of the first two races, because they must run without the advantage of well-rested competitors. Anyone who has ever spent time around children knows the visible and dramatic difference in a child's behavior when she/he is tired as opposed to when they are rested. (Just imagine a kindergarten without rest periods!) That need doesn't go away just because we get older. Some very progressive companies are now trying new ways to ensure that employees are rested; providing rest spaces or promoting various patterns of alternating work and rest times. I once had to do a presentation to employees in the oil fields of

Prudoe Bay on Alaska's North Slope. Most employees there work 12 hour shifts for two weeks and then have two weeks off, a schedule that acknowledges that hard work requires good long rest periods. And yet there persists among us some judgment of rest as negative. We need to disabuse ourselves of that notion and turn it completely upside down.

Make this a New Year's resolution—consider not doing something; simply create some small amount of time and space for rest, and build that into your schedule without judging yourself for doing so. Then, block that time into next December's calendar, and don't give it up for anything!

30

ELIMINATE THE WORD "SHOULD" FROM WHAT YOU EXPECT OF YOURSELF AND OTHERS.

Back when the New Age was new, at the dawn of the Age of Aquarius, many people explored a variety of mindsets and/or states of mind. "Don't should on me" became a catchphrase for some based on the availability of freedom from judgment in the broader cultural perspective of the day. The onerous nature of the word "should" was revealed to mean that either you or someone else was determining what you ought to do or be doing, whether that was your actual choice or preferred action. The phrase acknowledged that as inappropriate.

Well, yes, you should brush your teeth every day, but don't be imposing your own beliefs about what you or other people should or shouldn't do much beyond that. That's a core problem with trying to make everyone's Christmas perfect. You heap a mountain of "should" on yourself. You *should* have the perfect gift for everyone, you *should* clean the house from top to bottom before decorating (Heaven forbid a speck of dust mar the perfect scene), you *should* bake all thirty-five of your friends and family's best-loved cookies, you *should* make sure everything is beautifully wrapped, you *should* have a perfectly beautiful tree, and of course, you *should* be able to do it all with a smile. That is, you *should* in just a few weeks' time, accomplish all the tasks it would take a small army to do in several months.

Really?

The only thing you really *should* do is give up "shoulding" on yourself.

31

BELIEVING YOU CAN DO IT ALL IS SETTING YOURSELF UP FOR DISAPPOINTMENT.

The myth of "you can do it all, you can have it all" is a thing of the past. And a good thing that it is, too. At least one generation of women drove ourselves to distraction trying to live up to it. Never mind what the magazines say or show. Your life is NOT a magazine article. You don't live in a magazine life. You live a real life with real responsibilities and real people.

I think I may have mentioned this elsewhere, but do you really think you can produce the confections and decorations that glaze the covers of all commercial magazines from November through December? If you are like most people, you don't have the kitchen, house, money, time or staff to do that. Do you really think you can? Of course, they bank on the fact that you will be lured into thinking you can. And if you could, what would you be giving up to do it?

Fortunately, many people are now looking elsewhere for their fulfillment in life, realizing that it is more about finding a balance in their spiritual lives, their healthy habits, and in connecting with people. This is a gain, not a loss. If you want to set ambitious goals for yourself, set them in areas related to connecting, listening, sharing and loving. They will mean more and be remembered longer than your amazing flaming dessert. And, hasn't Chevy Chase taught us anything about decorating for Christmas? His movie disasters are funny, but somehow resonate with our own that aren't funny and can be pretty disastrous. Instead of setting yourself up for disaster, set yourself down and watch *Christmas Vacation* with your family. Make it a tradition. There's a pretty good chance you won't be disappointed.

32

ASK SOMEONE ELSE HOW THEY ARE COPING. LISTEN TO WHAT THEY SAY.

This one is important. You can make a difference to everyone you meet. Consider a typical holiday exchange:

"Hi, How are you?"

"Good. Good, thanks, how are you?"

"Good, thanks."

"Enjoying the holidays?"

"Sure, yeah, busy, but, you know."

"Yeah, I know. Really busy. Well, Merry Christmas!"

"Merry Christmas to you too!"

Nothing real has been said. Both parties are probably anxious to be done with each other and move on to some chore or errand. As I mentioned earlier, I have developed a habit of questioning people's responses to the question "How are you?" I know it must drive some of my friends crazy, but most of them know it's coming. It's probably the strangers who are really caught off guard. A typical exchange goes something like this:

Me: "Hi, how are you?"

Friend or Stranger: "Good, how are you?"

Me: "Good? You're just good? Not great? Not excellent?"

Friend or Stranger: "Well, you know, my rabbit got sick, and my boss is being a jerk about letting me take an extra day off around the holidays, and Suzie has a tournament we have to go to three days after Christmas and the tires on the car probably won't make it all the way, and (so on and so on.)"

It's really amazing what people will share in a brief exchange, and it's so easy to give them this opportunity to let you know how they are really doing. Even if they just say they are really busy, you can offer some sympathy or acknowledgement of their feelings with a comment like, "Wow, how are you coping?" You may be having a hard time, but so may they. Don't make "How are you?" about yourself. Mean it when you ask, and listen to the answer. Give someone the gift of your attention. Give them the chance to be real and to share and to be listened to.

33

STOP AND SMELL THE SPICES.

A rose may be a rose, and summer certainly has its wonderful floral fragrances, but Christmas has its own special scents that trigger delicious memories of spicy cinnamon or gingerbread cookies, eggnog with nutmeg, crisp snow-tinged air, evergreens, and peppermint candy canes. Twenty years ago, you pretty much needed the real thing to experience those scents, but today, you can just stop in at your local candle store or the candle/air freshener aisle of the supermarket and find these and many others in a variety of forms.

Cutting back on baking Christmas cookies? No problem. There are Christmas cookie scented candles. Got a fake tree? No problem. You can get candles, sprays, wax melts, plug-ins and even car air fresheners in a variety of evergreen scents. The same holds true for all the familiar favorites, and the ingenious manufacturers have also utilized the magic of chemistry to capture and create an endless variety of combinations of unique originals. You want cranberry apple? No problem. Balsam and cedar, bay leaf wreath, Winterberry (whatever that is)? You name it, they've got it. And, if you can't decide, there are always a few generics like *Christmas Eve*, or *Christmas Wreath* or *Snowman* to give you the olfactory ambiance you want.

Christmas scents are heartwarming like comfort food. It's so easy now to have them in your home at the flick of a match (or a switch). Use them to help escape the stress. Close your eyes and relax into them, and you can imagine any perfectly perfect scene you want around you.

34

DON'T FIGHT FOR CLOSE-IN PARKING. INSTEAD, ENJOY WALKING IN THE FRESH AIR.

Where I live, trying to walk in the fresh air around Christmastime might mean that gale-force winds with sheets of ice pellets will assault your progress. The ground might appear to be uneven because the snow that had been falling before has turned to ice and drifted. The ground probably will be uneven, no matter how perfectly flat the parking lot, because other people have walked or driven over it. If the temperature is between 15 and 30 degrees, the plows have likely scattered salt that melted some of the snow into a chilling slush that will leak through your leather boots, I don't care how many coats of water proofing spray you put on them in the fall. And the salt will also leave nasty puckered stains on the leather too. Below 15 degrees, you just have to deal with the ice because salt doesn't melt it.

This business of enjoying walking in winter is a tall order. Those gigantic parking lots are really full on Black Friday and at Christmastime, and we are not used to having to walk so far to get into stores. Of course, it's annoying to have to walk the length of the lot and even worse when you spot someone pulling out of a great spot and another car beats you to it. This is a formula for instant road rage, or parking lot rage as the case may be.

In retrospect, I think this suggestion may just have a tad too much of the Pollyanna in it. Oh, it's a great idea, but really? Let's make this weather-and-time dependent. Try it only if it is before dark (so, say noon to three) and when the weather is just lovely for a nice walk. After all, you might just save yourself a fender bender or a fight, and who needs either of those? If the weather is bad and it's dark and cold and scary, go home and order whatever you want online. You couldn't do that twenty years ago. Now you can. Merry Christmas!

35

WRAP NO MORE THAN FIVE PRESENTS AT A TIME.

A young man, whom I know well, attends the North Country School in New York's Adirondack Mountains, a boarding school that reminds me of 19th century Utopian communities. In addition to rigorous academic work, students participate in weekly rotations of chores. The most challenging of all assignments is barn chores, as these require getting up at 6:30 a.m., hiking the half mile to the barn, through deep winter snow in sub-freezing temperatures before breakfast to feed and water the assorted livestock and to collect, wash, count and store the eggs. (Can't you just hear him telling his grandchildren, "When I was a boy...") Here's the thing: he loves it and loves doing it with his friends, and by all accounts, he is always on time for chores and does them willingly and enthusiastically, aware of the importance of each job to the welfare of the entire community. He works happy.

In contrast, last summer he found himself to be a little short of pocket cash and decided to offer up his services to mow a few lawns. Let's just say that something told me his heart wasn't entirely in this job. Was it the teenaged long face? Was it the slumped shoulders? Was it the half run at which he pushed the mower to get the job done, cutting a few corners along the way? It doesn't really matter. He didn't really want to mow the lawn. He just wanted the money for mowing the lawn. What matters is how he experienced the work.

Wrapping presents may seem like a delightfully creative and leisurely experience, but sometimes, it becomes the lawn we don't really want to mow. We don't really want to wrap. We just want beautifully wrapped packages we can be proud of, and we try to make that happen without enough time or energy. I love real cloth ribbon and colorful papers, but wrapping five packages is my limit. Yours may be different. You may be one of those people who revels in tissue and tape with the Origami skill of precision folds. After five, I'm ready for that greatest of all wrapping shortcuts – the gift bag. That makes me work happy. Don't let the job of wrapping suck the joy out of giving.

By the way, when alumni return to that school for visits, more than anything else, they want to participate in barn chores. Wrap happy. You will look forward to the chore in the future.

36

PONDER GENUINE JOY.

We see the word "joy" everywhere at Christmas—on cards, gift wrap, and giant banners across storefronts hoping for joyful bottom lines. We sing "Joy to the World" at church, but do we ever really think about genuine joy? Of course everybody is happy in church, smiling broadly while singing celebratory songs. That's joyful, but when I think about real, bone-deep, take-your-breath-away joy, I think of something that goes way beyond happy. There is joy at weddings. There is joy associated with victories or achievements of one sort or another; there is joy in music and in a sunrise or a beautiful sunset.

The most profound joy I have ever witnessed or experienced was at the very moment of a baby's birth—when my daughter was born, and when her son was born. Both times, there was an exhilarating and complicated rush of feeling so powerful that it did in fact catch my breath and bring tears to my eyes, laughter to my lips, peace and relief to my mind, joy and love to my heart.

The wait was over. The labor was over. The mother and baby were fine. This little person who wasn't a visible reality before suddenly became one. There was a new life among us.

Imagine when that baby was Jesus! That joy is what the songs are about, what Christians can feel at Christmas. It's beyond the amazing joy that one family shares when witnessing a birth. It's a joy for the whole of humankind to share. It's the joy of what they have been waiting for over generations. That's a feeling worth pondering and worth feeling. I wish you that kind of joy at Christmas.

37

RECOGNIZE THAT PERFECTION IS A DIRECTION, NOT A GOAL.

Perfect is such an absolute. There is no perfecter and perfectest. Things are either perfect or imperfect. I guess we can say we want something to be *"more nearly perfect,"* or, as the framers of our United States Constitution said they were hoping for, "a *more perfect* union." But none of that sounds quite right, so it seems odd to call it a direction. It would seem that perfect is indeed a goal, but I think it is an unattainable one and that's what I meant here.

It is, perhaps, specifically perfection in all things Christmas that makes "perfect" a problem for me. It gets all mixed up with expectations and what your vision of perfect might be compared to mine, and so on. I do sincerely believe that trying to make Christmas perfect can ruin it, because trying too hard makes it all a big chore or contest to outdo your neighbor's light show or your grandmother's cookie production or maybe the White House gingerbread house. If the definition of perfect is something like a picture painted by Norman Rockwell, well folks, those were pictures from the imagination of one man, in other words, fiction. If it is what you see on TV with all the happy families and glamorous couples dressed to the nines, well, those are commercials, concoctions to make you believe you can recreate your own life into something like that just by buying those products. If your definition is to have a warm and wonderful time, enjoying the people and spirit of the season, without making yourself crazy or going into debt, well then, your definition matches mine.

38

SMILE ANYWAY.

This year, I'm giving the Smile Anyway Award to a woman I encountered on an Amtrak train while on vacation in July. The train had stopped at Fort Edward, New York, along the beautiful Adirondack route, and my seatmate was disembarking there. Just as she reached the exit, halfway down the car, I realized that she had left her reusable lunch container in the seat pocket. I grabbed it and hurried forward into the aisle, hoping to catch her, but not noticing an obstacle. Was it a bag on the floor? Was it the man who stood up on my right? Whatever it was, it caught my foot and sent me sailing, swan-dive style, through the air. It was one of those accidents that happen in a flash but you experience in slow motion, and I only wish I had a video of myself, airborne in full Superman pose. I would love to see the expression on my face when I realized that the woman I was about to land on was dressed entirely in white and holding a very full plastic cup of very brown cola with ice. The splatter pattern we shared will remain one of my most vivid memories. She took the bigger hit on that one, as the cup landed in her lap.

At that point, I was surrounded with a 360 chorus of kindly passengers and train staff asking, "Are you alright?" even before I could determine if I indeed was. Even the woman in white asked with concern, "Did you hit your eye?" and I responded, "No," although I did, in fact, hit the arm rest and sported a shiner and a small cut on my brow for the week after.

That woman was so gracious, so concerned about me and so unconcerned about herself, that I was even more embarrassed, as I apologized profusely and made my way back to sink into my seat.

Two friendly Amtrak conductors saw to both of us, bringing me an ice pack for my knee and helping her to retrieve her bag and find a place to change into something dry and "uncola." What clenched the Smile Anyway Award for her was when I overheard someone in her party comment about the incident, and she shrugged it off, replying, "It's all part of the adventure."

So, let's hear it for the lady in white, whoever you are, wherever you are. Congratulations. And may we all strive to compete with your excellent performance for this, your well-deserved honor, during the holiday season and throughout the year.

39

RING BELLS.

There is joy in the ring and the ringing of bells, and Christmas is the most joyous time of year. Historically and culturally, bells have meant many things, from the exciting proclamation of joyous occasions, to the slow tolling announcement of grief, or the calling together of people in times of crisis or at a time to worship.

While electronic and digital imitations emanate from all too many towers, some older churches, including one in my town, still have bell towers with long ropes and dedicated ringers. Families can sign up to be bell ringers here, the most coveted time slot being at midnight on Christmas Eve.

If you don't have access to an opportunity to heft one of these kinds of ropes, I would suggest you try something smaller. You could join a bell choir, or volunteer to be a bell ringer for the Salvation Army. You don't have to wear a red Santa suit.

You can also just make bells a part of your decorations and customs. I have bells hung on doorknobs in my house and wind chimes hung in doorways. I love the tinkling, ringing sounds that punctuate the quiet with joy.

Bells are a big part of Christmas. "Sleigh bells ring, are you listening,…","Silver bells, silver bells, it's Christmas time in the city…", "Jingle bells, jingle bells, jingle all the way…", "I heard the bells on Christmas day, their old, familiar carols play, and wild and sweet the words repeat of peace on earth, good-will to men!"

Ring them.

40

TRY TO RECALL THE MAGIC OF CHILDHOOD.

Most of life is magical to little children. So much just happens without their input or effort. Things just happen, as if by magic. Santa Claus delivering presents via the chimney at night is no more unbelievable than the lights coming on in the house or ice forming on the pond. And we adults love to perpetuate the magic of Santa, perhaps because we are the ones who have to produce the magic. Don't give up on that. Recall and perpetuate the magic of childhood for every child you know or encounter. Read *The Polar Express* to them. Teach them to believe, because the magic doesn't go away as they grow older. It just changes.

The childlike wonder-producing sense of the magic of Christmas may be exactly what we are trying to recreate or capture for ourselves when we embark on massive efforts to produce a perfect Merry Christmas for everyone, sometimes at the expense of our own sleep if not sanity. Surely, we can create the magic for our children. That doesn't take much. They are already believers. But instead of trying recreate the same scenario as adults, I think we need to see it as it is and understand the magic in that. It is an opportunity to care for others and to show we care. There is magic in that, even if it's just hauling yourself out of bed and getting the Pop Tarts into the toaster before your coffee is ready. You give someone a quarter for a parking meter, or allow them the right of way on the road. You donate to charity or volunteer your time. You care. You are showing it by doing something for someone else. That's sharing the love, the deep, continuing, important kind. That's the real magic of Christmas.

41

CONSIDER A FAKE TREE.

Reduce, reuse, recycle. I really hate this idea when it comes to a Christmas tree. Of all the traditions we love to maintain, few are as central to our holiday as the Christmas tree, and the real tree is the best and the highest standard—the bigger the better, and the more heavily laden with what we consider traditional decorations, the better.

I love big, beautiful, fully decked out trees, and they do bring back wonderful childhood memories. People love to bring a real tree into the house in winter. I do too. But, my top reasons for not having a real tree are:

- ❖ They are too beautiful for me to kill for my few weeks of enjoyment.

- ❖ They are very expensive.

- ❖ I could use that money elsewhere, perhaps charitably.

- ❖ They are hard to set up and decorate.

❖ They make a mess.

Besides all that, real trees are becoming increasingly fake, as they are farmed, pruned, and cut so far in advance of Christmas to make it to market on time, that they are often sprayed with some unnatural green colored stuff to make them look fresh. Here's a clue to freshness. The branches shouldn't be too stiff when you touch them, and they should have a strong evergreen smell. Absent that, you are not getting anything much different than a fake. If you make getting the tree a family outing and have fun getting it together, then ignore this suggestion. If not, reconsider.

My solution has been to drop down to a tabletop-sized tree. I still hate killing them, but rationalize that another one can grow that big in just a few years. Besides, it fits through the door without making a mess, is cheaper, and is less likely to topple over, and doesn't take much to decorate beautifully.

42

LEARN TO LET GO OF LITTLE RESENTMENTS.

Come on, you know you have them; that toy your sister/brother borrowed and broke, that comment your mother-in-law made on your wedding day, the raise your colleague got for something you helped do. We had a very interesting discussion about forgiveness at church one day. It became very clear that the person who you think wronged you probably doesn't even remember the "wrong," if they were ever even aware of it. So, they aren't carrying the burden that you are. You are actually making yourself suffer while they have moved on and are having a perfectly good time of it. That doesn't sound fair, but the only way to fix it is for you to break that chain that is tying you to them in resentment and pulling you down.

This could actually be a very nice gift you could give yourself. Think about it. What good is that resentment doing you? Are you nurturing it, holding it and making it grow by watching for any evidence that it could become bigger. Step away from this place and let go of those resentments. Therapists have lots of methods to help you do this. Write the wrong on a piece of wood and throw it in the fire. Write it on a helium balloon and send it off into the thin air. I kind of like the idea of just staring at a mirror and saying something to yourself like, "I like you and don't want to see you carry this burden any longer. Forget about it." You could follow that with a daily mantra every time you see yourself in the mirror—something positive and uplifting to the effect that you are happy to be free of whatever.

Christmas would be a great time to give yourself that gift, and you would be much happier.

> Joy and resentment can not co-exist.
> Henri J. M. Nouwen, *The Return of the Prodigal Son: A Story of Homecoming*

43

STIR COCOA WITH CANDY CANES.

Lord, I don't think we have figured out yet how to manage the blessing of the cocoa plant, unless it's one of those choice things where there's both good and evil and we just have to face up to our own tastes, our dietary responsibilities and tendencies towards obesity. Chocolate and that penultimate comfort food, hot chocolate, are clearly gifts from God that recent research shows is nothing short of a brilliant creation. Like chocolate, cocoa is now being found to have health benefits.

My mother used to make hot cocoa for my sister, brother and me every morning before school in winter. It was a process of pure love. It was not just a matter of pouring hot water into a pouch of powder emptied into a cup. She steamed milk and carefully measured the cocoa and sugar and mixed them well and filled our mugs and brought them to the table when the temperature was just right. Sometimes, she would even add a dollop of real home-made whipped cream.

It was only when I was older that I discovered there were other interesting things that would enhance cocoa, and peppermint, another old medicinal product, turned out to be one of my favorites.

When my grandson was staying with me this year, we got snowed in one day, and I suggested maybe a nice cup of hot cocoa was in order. I also suggested that he might want to try stirring it with a peppermint stick which he did, enthusiastically. Not one to miss the chance to make a good thing better, he decided to add a couple of marshmallows and then some whipped cream. He was thrilled with the concoction and I refrained from indicating my preference for a simpler version. No matter what the ingredients, nothing really matters quite as much as the simple pleasures of the wonderful time spent anticipating, preparing and enjoying the drink.

44

TOLERATE PRETENSION,
BUT DON'T PRACTICE IT.

I believe in saving face, although I know that many younger people would disagree with that and say that you ought to confront, or to "call people out." So, if you are at a lovely little posh neighborhood Christmas party, and the host, Mr. Biggesthouseontheblock, is going on about the high quality of the expensive artwork on his walls and you happen to know that the antique shop where he bought it sells nothing but fakes, what do you do? Do you smile and nod and look like you believe what he believes, or do you say, "Didn't you buy that painting at *Trader Knows* where the guy was written up in the paper for dealing exclusively with that famous art forger?" This latter choice might be endorsed by the "confront" team, but it might also prove to be a real conversation stopper. I mean, where do you go from there? The basic rule of party talk is the same as the basic rule for improvisation: you must not say anything that will stop the conversation.

Thus, I would recommend you tolerate any similar incident of pretension. It's not really hurting you, even if the speaker seems to think she/he is demonstrating his/her own superior knowledge, taste, social class or economic status. The fact is, you are "in the know," and they are not. This might be a good time to assume a benign smile and search the faces of anyone else hearing this talk to look for clues that they too might be debating what might be the most morally responsible reaction to have at that point. Or, it might be a good time to decide to go refill your glass or perhaps a good time to go home.

A pretentious person is rather like a person who has over-imbibed while everyone else has exhibited a certain amount of propriety or restraint or got to the party late. She/he is unknowingly embarrassing the heck out of him or herself. Pretension is a weakness. Watch out for it. Learn from it. Don't practice it, because if you do, there will likely be someone listening with a benign smile and a stone-cold sense of your foolishness.

45

USE REAL RIBBON AND SAVE IT FOR NEXT YEAR.

I love real ribbon, especially the smooth satin kind with crimped edges (any width from petite to broad) and the ridged jewel-toned grosgrain, hair-ribbon kind. Those are my favorite, although the numbers of kinds of ribbon have exploded like fireworks in past years. There's translucent ribbon, sequined ribbon, paper ribbon, curly ribbon, hemp ribbon, and ribbon with wire in the edges so you can shape a bow without actually knowing how to tie it. The choices are many.

Anyone who has ever shopped in Europe knows that wrapping is taken very seriously there. Even the smallest purchase might come in a delightfully adorned package. I once purchased something relatively inexpensive in Switzerland. It might have been a box of chocolates, or maybe a Christmas ornament. It was very elaborately wrapped by the sales clerk, far beyond what you might expect and something to behold. There was the lovely paper wrapped with precision folds, and then on top there was a gold printed paper fan topped with a nest of something that looked like gold steel wool. Tucked into that was a sprig of something else, and all of it was tied up neatly under two different kinds of ribbon. One might almost have been tempted not to unwrap it. What a joy it was to present that gift!

Clearly, that kind of elaborate packaging is not something I would recommend attempting on a routine basis. But there is something about the lure of real ribbon that makes a wrapped gift far more appealing than, say, a gift bag or a machine-made plastic bow stuck on a box. You know the kind I mean—the ones that never really stay stuck on.

I have a respect for real ribbon. It is woven. You use your own hands to cut and tie it. It is a bit of beautiful color and tradition that can be rolled up and reused, carrying with it the memories of many years. I don't really think it takes that much more effort to use real ribbon rather than to slap on a bow from a bag when you have to peel backing off, stick the bow on and then likely tape it on as well. Real ribbon feels good in your hands, and you can use the time you are tying it to think about the person who will untie it. Over and over again.

46

MAKE MERRY.

What a concept! We keep wishing each other "Merry Christmas!" but it seems to have become little more than a seasonal greeting. Does it really convey a hope for being joyous, mirthful and gay? The word *merry* has been around since the Middle Ages, its meaning and frequency of use fluctuating over time.

Here is a definition of merry:

<u>cheerful and lively</u>

synonyms: cheerful, cheery, in high spirits, high-spirited, bright, sunny, smiling, lighthearted, buoyant, lively, carefree, without a care in the world, joyful, joyous, jolly, convivial, festive, mirthful, gleeful, happy, glad, laughing

<u>antonym: miserable</u>

(https://www.google.com/search?q=merry&ie=utf-8&oe=utf-&aq=t&rls=org.mozilla:en-US:official&client=firefox-a&channel=sb retrieved 7/18/14)

Maybe this is a central thought. If we focus on the *Merry* in

Christmas, how happy we are at this miraculous time, our feelings at the moment–ours and others, perhaps that will help move our thoughts and actions from the panic of production, the setting up a kind of three-ring Christmas circus with the decorations, food and gifts being the rings, to something much merrier. It's hard to be cheerful and lively when setting up a three-ring circus. It's too exhausting.

Think *Merry* Christmas and say *Merry* Christmas with *cheerful* and *lively* and all those other synonyms on your mind and then go make merry—be cheerful and lively and all those other synonyms. Don't be an antonym.

I wish you a Merry Christmas!
I wish you a Merry Christmas!
I wish you a Merry Christmas!

47

FOCUS INWARD WHEN ALONE,
OUTWARD WHEN WITH OTHERS.

This is an incredibly complicated matter, and includes questions on whether you are an introvert or an extrovert and just how mentally stable you are feeling at the moment. When I first suggested this, I meant that it's important to remember "It's not all about me" when interacting with other people.

I know I am guilty of forgetting this. I am a guilty grandma—that is, guilty of talking too much about my only grandson, although I do try to monitor myself in that direction. I am reminded of the old adage "Never ask a farmer about pigs," the point being that you will hear far more about pigs than you care to. Never ask me about my grandson.

Check in with people you encounter around Christmas. It's a stressful time. Let them know that you really are interested in how they are and that you do care about them. Love is the message of Christmas, and *Love thy neighbor* carries a truckload of meaning in ring-box sized sentence. Try to avoid "How are you?" in favor of something more specific. Ask about their family, their job, their holiday plans or anything else you might remember that could be important to them, like "How's that goldfish you won at the fair?" The point is to give people an opportunity to really share something and to really share yourself with them by turning off your impulse to speak and to listen instead.

On the flip side, don't hesitate to respond with sincerity when someone asks, "How are you?" especially if you can do it in 25 words or less. You will know right away if the question was sincere based on the reaction you get. Their eyes will either light up or glaze over. You will know who really cares how you are. Be one who cares.

48

EXPECT ANY ADVERTISED SPECIAL
TO BE SOLD OUT.

Most years, I have managed to avoid shopping at all on the annual open-season for consumers, BF (Black Friday). There have been a few occasions, however, when a romanticized notion of joining the fun, getting a great buy and perhaps having lunch with a friend or family member on a day off, have clouded my perception of reality to the point that I ventured out. I was astounded at what I saw and experienced. It was not just the impossibility of finding a parking space (some folks get quite creative in this area, others get quite combative), long lines of impatient people, battles for shopping carts, and family members teaming up on cell phones to expand their success rate at grabbing all the specials before running off to the next store. There was also a desperation that made me think the stakes were much higher than the price. It was as if life itself depended on the success of the shopping trip, and that success permitted the careless abandonment of any of the normally assumed rules of social orderliness. People who might ordinarily hold open a door for each other, smile, or simply yield a pedestrian right-of-way were now acting in ways they might later be quite embarrassed to see on screen if videos were taken. On one day, everyone became the bully in the Easter Egg hunt. It was too startling and too depressing for me. I left without buying anything, and even knowing that was my choice, I couldn't help feeling like a failure. I didn't measure up to the task. I was the loser.

When Black Friday turned fatal a few years back, the tragedy caused some stores to start trying to come up with ideas to lower the risk of the day's madness for customers. There were guarantees of the availability of "doorbuster"-priced products and sales that started as early as Thanksgiving evening. Some stores began staying open all night, but still there was the press of crowds and the prevalence of incidents.

The time has come for manufacturers and stores to really step up to the plate here. What if they didn't do deep discounts? The great shopping competition is really just a side effect of the great selling competition. Can merchants and manufacturers really celebrate their profit margins when a shopper dies in the press of a crowd? What sort of moral depravity is that? What if all manufacturers refused to allow discounting of their products?

I'm afraid that it is really only we, the customers, who are in control and able to change things. The fact is that if we don't participate, the practice will stop. Only we can prevent BF madness. None of us can change mass behavior alone, but we can change ourselves. If you must shop on BF, don't get crazed over the advertised special. If you happen to score it, consider yourself lucky. If you don't get it, but you get away unharmed or without harming anyone else, consider yourself even luckier. Better yet, stay away from any stores that support this madness.

49

UNDERSTAND THAT ALCOHOL
IS WORSE THAN ICE ON THE HIGHWAY.

According to the National Highway Traffic Safety Administration, "Alcohol-impaired motor vehicle crashes cost more than an estimated $37 billion annually." I don't know how they estimate that number. I guess it might be a combination of property damage costs and emergency services utilized. MADD estimates it at over $130 billion. But the incalculable cost is in human lives lost or impacted. NHTSA reported more than 10,000 fatalities in alcohol-impaired driving crashes - one every 51 minutes, in 2012.

A truly sobering (forgive the pun) website is maintained by alcoholalert.com It is the "Death Clock," showing the total number of drunk driving deaths this year (so far) in the U.S. In mid July, 2014, it was at 5172. So, unless things slow down in the next six months, this would suggest that increased safety features in cars and increased alcohol awareness, have not significantly lowered the death rate in the past few years, and a whole lot of families and friends will soon feel the impact.

This is not an easy subject to write about, or a pleasant thing to consider. But it is a reality we can't deny. Any one of us who loses a loved one because we or someone else over-imbibed will live with the horrendous pain of that preventable loss for the rest of our lives. No drink is worth that, and we need to do whatever we can to prevent it. It seems such an easy fix to monitor our consumption and to monitor each other for this when the stakes are so high.

50

CHECK STORES FOR EXPANDED HOURS AND SHOP ONLY IN THE VERY EARLY AND VERY LATE ONES.

This may be the best kept secret of the Christmas shopping season, and it's not because the merchants haven't advertised it. They blast the news of their expanded hours all over their ads. And yet, these odd hours seem to remain undersubscribed.

There was a suburban mall not far from where I worked for many years at a major university medical center. I started work at eight in the morning, and the big stores opened at seven around Christmas. Five days a week, I got close-in parking, attentive, if sleepy clerks, no waiting lines, and crowd-free aisles to browse. I never had to take a day off work to try to get all my shopping done. It became a leisurely process of finding something (or maybe nothing) each day, but I got to enjoy doing it.

I never did check the late night hours. I like to go sleep early at night. I know that not everybody can take advantage of these times. There are kids to put on school buses and jobs that start even earlier (like in stores and medical centers), but if it is at all possible, I would recommend trying this. It really is a wonderful way to get to shop and enjoy the festive decorations without the grief and with a great parking spot.

Of course, if it's absolutely impossible, you can also shop from home 24/7. Twenty years ago, shopping from home was most often dependent on someone answering the phone during business hours. Now, not so much. You can shop your heart out all night long, if you want without requiring retail staff to work insane hours. This suggestion may need to be modified to "Shop online."

51

GIVE OF YOURSELF,
BUT DON'T GIVE UP YOURSELF.

Here is the heart of the quandary that I struggle with. I truly believe that most of what we do to try to make Christmas perfect is done out of love for others. We want to make the people we love happy, but that's tricky.

There are some issues here. First, do we really have the power to do that? Second, we buy things, we make things, and we give things. Keyword here: *things*. That's a clue. Things are not really what make us happy. I once saw a woman receive a beautifully wrapped gift of jewelry from a man sitting across a dining table from her. He handed her the small blue box from an expensive and well-known jewelry store. She opened it carelessly and without comment. She looked at it, then put it aside on the table and went on eating. I don't know what might have been going on between them, but this incident happened over fifty years ago, and yet, I can still recall it. I was stunned to learn that something so precious could be so worthless.

If it is not the things that matter, what does? We say, "It's the thought that matters." Time may be the most precious thing we have, so spending it thinking of someone else does have value. Spending it with someone else would have even more value. What we give others is only a thing, unless it is our time. What we do for others is giving of ourselves, but if we get carried away, we can destroy the value of that by destroying ourselves. Our selves are what our loved ones care for. They don't want us to work all night or chase around for the perfect gift or spend so much that we will have financial problems and end up exhausted. If you care enough to give to a loved one, understand that they care for you and want you to care for yourself as well.

52

SAVE AT LEAST THREE EVENINGS A WEEK TO WRAP GIFTS AND WRITE CARDS.

Wow! How did I ever imagine that anyone could set aside three whole evenings a week? This is a tough one. Parties, shopping, baking, bills, dinner, school pageants/concerts/games, colds, whatever! What an incredibly ambitious goal! I can't believe that anyone could set aside three whole nights a week for anything. The problem is, these things (wrapping gifts and writing cards) do seem to need to get done at holiday time, but you can't make the time and so you can't do it all, so what can you do?

My sister used to have an elaborate ritual related to writing Christmas cards. I don't recall the details, but in my mind's eye, it went something like this:

She had her cards, envelopes, address book, Christmas music CDs, fountain pen (yes, that's what she used), return address labels and Christmas stamps and all ready and in one place by early November.

She waited until the weather conditions were perfect. That meant there would be a gently falling snow.

She took all her supplies and a nice cup of Christmas mint tea, turned on the music, sat at a table by the window and personally penned long greetings on each of her cards.

What a lovely picture, a lovely process, and what a lovely time she had of it, although this activity was very dependent on the right weather at the right time and sometimes things didn't all work out quite as she had hoped, like the year it only rained almost until Christmas. Alas, she has since succumbed to the Christmas letter habit, printing off copies of a word-processed review of the year's activities of her, her husband, and her many children and grandchildren. That's around fifteen people counting in-laws, partners and grandchildren, so who could blame her?

The point I was trying to make when I first wrote this suggestion was only this: that if you intend to send cards and wrap packages, figure out when the Dickens you are going to do that. Be realistic. This stuff doesn't just happen by itself. I, for one, have forgone cards in certain years, more than once. Cards are a lovely tradition. I hope you make time to write them; send me one too. Just don't forget that (like wrapping packages) it takes time. (Sis, I love you, but I have to admit that I don't read the Christmas letter right away. After all, it's Christmas. I love the news, but I read it in January, as a kind of retrospective look at the family's last year at the beginning of the New Year. A simple Merry Christmas In your own delightful left-handed script is lovely at Christmas, and enough.)

53

MAKE SNOW ANGELS.

Wouldn't it just be super cool if everyone went out and made snow angels every time it snowed? Or snow wo/men? OK, not possible for everyone, but you get the gist of this, don't you? It smacks of embracing the situation you are in, doing something fun and silly and childlike and doing it with abandon, never mind the snow that slips into your boots and mittens. Making a snow creature would be another good choice. We have seen some really creative ones in recent years. Do something nonessential and non-productive and loving of what little things life has to offer even under challenging conditions. Maybe where you live it means making sand angels on the beach or writing "Merry Christmas" in the sand or building a sand Christmas tree or critter. Whatever.

If ever there is a time of year to feel the joy of living, this is it. If you are housebound, maybe you could make a popcorn necklace, or cut a chain of paper dolls out of newspapers or make paper snowflakes. It doesn't matter anymore if you don't remember how to do these things, because now there are great instructions on how to do anything on YouTube. Or you could just sit and read a Christmas book or watch a Christmas movie. The real challenge of any of these activities is to let yourself do them. It requires that you release yourself from any other obligation or stress for sufficient time to just have some fun. Maybe it's even something brief and small and spontaneous, like trying to slide across a frozen puddle rather than balancing on tiptoe around it. It's about appreciating letting go and letting yourself have fun and feel the joy.

Be silly. Be honest. Be kind.
Ralph Waldo Emerson

54

DON'T SHOP FOR FRIENDS
ON YOUR LUNCH HOUR.
GO TO LUNCH WITH YOUR FRIENDS

I really love this idea. Go to lunch with your friends, or better yet, dinner if possible, so you really have some time to spend together. If it has to be lunch, then follow these steps:

❖ Try to arrange a long lunch hour.

❖ Pick a place nearby that has the best food, service and atmosphere.

❖ Make a reservation.

❖ Check this idea out with your friend ahead of time and see if she/he doesn't also love the idea of spending time together rather than feeling the need to purchase something for exchange.

❖ Extract a promise not to bring a gift anyway and to turn off your phones during lunch. A gift and a phone would defeat the purpose of setting this time and money aside. There is really nothing more precious that any of us has or can give to each other than our time.

❖ Don't cancel or change this date for anything short of a medical emergency.

❖ Keep the conversation focused on each other and on your friendship.

❖ Affirm that this beats wondering what the other would like as a gift and shopping for it.

The best part about this is that it doesn't really have to be an either/or (gift or time) if that works for you. If you have the time, know your friend well and you both have already say, knit each other a pair of alpaca socks in your favorite color, so much the better. If not, go for the lunch, not the gift. But don't let the lunch be a slap dash, quickly dealt with obligation. Make it a special time to be together.

55

ADOPT A LARGER PERSPECTIVE.

Not a whole lot of stuff looks better close up. Okay, maybe those snowflakes I was talking about earlier, but not much else. You might step up to a painting to get a close look at the brushstrokes, but to really see the picture and appreciate it, you have to step back.

Take a step back when considering your Christmas. Look at the whole picture. When dealing with each and every aspect of the holiday, each and every detail, measure it against its relative importance to the whole of your holiday. Does every single strand of tinsel really have to hang straight down? Does every single dish on the Christmas dinner table have to be gourmet? Is this a major crisis, or is this a little crisis in relation to the whole of the holiday?

When you are finished considering each detail in relation to the whole of your holiday, consider the holiday as a whole in relation to the year, your life and the lives of others. Stay on this track until you've got a bird's eye view, or even higher, a satellite, Google Earth global perspective. What if we all looked at the world like this day by day and remembered always that we are all members of the same entire global family? Christmas is the perfect time to start.

Oh, dear Lord, these things I pray.

Lyrics by John Farmham

56

LAUGH LIKE SANTA.
PROMISE YOURSELF ONE GOOD LAUGH A DAY.

I listed these two thoughts separately in my first book. They seem now to be getting at the same idea, although the Santa part is a bit odd.

What do you suppose Santa is laughing at? It's really a little bizarre and creepy-clown-like and may be why so many kids cry on his lap at the mall. It probably wouldn't really be advisable to hold your belly and roar out a rollicking "Ho, Ho, Ho" in any public place or even among friends, unless you are trying out for the holiday mall job.

Most sources tell us that laughter is good for your health. My Dad had a booming laugh. The local high school used to give him free tickets to their comedy shows because he could always get the whole audience laughing. It wasn't fake either. He would just burst out with a huge chain of laughs. We always knew when he was in the audience, and where he was in the audience as well.

My father-in-law also had a good hearty laugh. In fact, he would get to laughing so hard sometimes at his own stories that he could no longer speak. This was especially true throughout the fall months when, after dinner each Sunday, he sampled the cherries he had marinating in Jack Daniels for Christmas to see how they were progressing. Apparently, it was necessary to sample quite a few.

I don't think anyone needs to have such a noteworthy laugh. I think the important thing is to not forget about it at Christmas. Maybe that's why Santa laughs—to remind us to do so. Laughter does tend to be infectious. Laughter means fun and relaxation and often turns up in the strangest places when people need to relieve stress. Think of the things that make you laugh and pursue them. Doing this as a family is best. Whether it's a favorite holiday movie, a game, a pillow fight or whatever, just do it. Make it a tradition. Make it a habit.

57

SYMPATHIZE WITH A STORE CLERK.

Really? Would you even consider trading places with this person? Sure, they may have been snippy with you, or decided to first serve the guy who cut in line in front of you-the one who said, "Excuse me, I just have a question," and proceeded to occupy the clerk for the next fifteen minutes. These things happen. They happen more often than we would hope, particularly when hoards of temporary, inexperienced sales associates are hired to cover the expanded holiday store hours. And sometimes their offenses really do seem like their fault.

It's easy to criticize. Some of what makes it hard to sympathize or empathize is our own feelings of entitlement, our territoriality, our own stress level. This may be the best time to show some Christmas cheer. Imagine what it might mean for someone to hear a kind word rather than a complaint. Lighten up in line. Consider what that person might be up against that requires them to work long hours, standing, and being full-time customer servant. Thank goodness for these people. Thank them for keeping the store open and processing your sale. Break into song to cheer up other customers while standing in line. "God rest ye merry gentlemen, let nothing you dismay."

I suspect you will be surprised by the reaction you get. (Disclaimer: Don't hold me responsible. I have never actually tried this and would also be surprised. Please let me know what happens if you try it. helen_I_thomas@hotmail.com)

58

TRY TO ENJOY YOUR GUESTS,
NOT IMPRESS THEM.

This is what was missing that very Christmas that I walked into my aunt's house and was confronted with her frustration at trying to make everything perfect. Giving her the benefit of the doubt, I would say that she genuinely wanted us all to be pleased, relaxed, happy and enjoying her hospitality. I want to believe that, but I can't help thinking that maybe somewhere in her head, a place that she may or not have been aware of, there were a few grains of thought about how impressed we would all be with her perfect tree, perfect meal and perfect gifts. Either way, what she did was to put a whole lot of effort (and time and money) into an event that turned on her.

It's nearly impossible to host a family Christmas and not have a lot of work to do. But when I think back on that time, I realize that she never asked anyone to bring a dish or a bottle of wine or a pie. She did all the food purchase and preparation herself, including a tasty variety of homemade cookies. Neither had we drawn names to exchange gifts at her house. She had purchased and wrapped a gift for each and every one of us, and she had decorated her house and her tree by herself as well. She had tried to do it all herself, and in fact she had done it. The downside was that she had done it at such a cost to herself that it impacted the rest of us too.

I don't mean to say that people shouldn't put effort into making Christmas a good time for everyone. It is a wonderful time—as the song says, "the most wonderful time of the year." I just want everybody to find some balance in the joy of it all and not get caught up in the downside. Enjoy. Enjoy everyone. Enjoy it all.

59

REMEMBER THAT ADS ARE DESIGNED TO CREATE DESIRE.

My agent told me once about writing, "Remember, you are not selling shoes, you are selling beautiful feet." I don't exactly know how that related to my writing, but the saying and its message have stayed with me, and I think that is exactly what the advertisers are doing to us all the time, especially at Christmas when we are all thinking about being loved and making others merry.

What do you see in the toy ads? Happy kids. What do you see in the game ads? Family fun (often at the expense of the bumbling dad, who loses the game. Isn't it fun to make dad look dumb?) And how about the jewelry ads? Love, of course. The engagement ring aimed at the younger hopefuls, the forever diamond whatever aimed at those who have been together forever, and those thousands of possible beads for every occasion from the brand-name bracelet companies that make beads to let you know you are loved.

I'm not saying don't buy those things. I don't want to be stalked by manufacturers and mall cops. All I'm saying is that it might be wise to know what your feet look like, in or out of those beautiful shoes. Be aware. Know when you are being sold something intangible and ask yourself if your expectations are realistic. This is particularly tricky with children. Marketers are ruthless in creating demand for toys that didn't even exist the year before and might well end up in the garage sale before the year is out. You can try to talk to your children about this, but I'm not sure you can expect them to understand, depending on their age. If it were up to me, all advertising would be banned in November and December. I truly wonder how that would impact the Chinese and our economy, not to mention our peace of mind.

Stand down, all you retailers and economists. There is not the remotest possibility that what I write will change anything. I'm just suggesting that people think a bit about it. You can call off the mall cops.

60

BE OF CHARITABLE SPIRIT.

This doesn't mean to drop a dollar in the bellringer's red bucket outside the department store, although that's not a bad idea. Nor is it something to be reserved only for the Christmas season. Clearly, the holidays are a time when we receive appeals from every imaginable charitable organization. (Did you get the one from PAWS the Performing Animals Welfare Society?) The need is real for each and the appeal is strong from each. It is a time of year when we are all thinking about giving, and the requestors are good at describing the need which is so much greater than our own. I usually give in and write a check, regardless of where else I routinely give and regardless of how small a check it is. But being of charitable spirit has different connotations in different contexts—not necessarily having to do with money at all—but maybe having to do more with random acts of kindness.

One time, when my daughter was working in Budapest and was new to streetcars as a method of transportation, she hopped on one just before it started up, and her foot got stuck in the closing door. She would have been sprawled on the grubby floor of the streetcar until the next stop, except that two older women stepped forward and supported her until the door opened again, and that without her being able to speak a word of their language.

It's about kindness and people are paying it forward, whether in favors or in fast food drive-throughs these days. It would be downright amazing if we could all consider and try to practice that kind of kindness every day.

On the question of charitable giving, see Peter J. Singer's, 2006 New York Times article *What Should a Billionaire Give and What Should You*? He says it best.

61

COMPLIMENT EVERY FIFTH PERSON YOU SEE.

Don't ask me why I suggested complimenting every *fifth* person you see. That certainly seems an arbitrary number. If it had some significance to me twenty years ago, that has been lost in the mists of time and misty memory. It would be nice to compliment *every* person you saw. Still, this conjures up in my mind a rather odd vision of someone chasing around the sidewalk to accost each person on it long enough to express something nice to them with a few words. This might elicit a very negative response from strangers, so perhaps the number five is fine, or maybe it should be a matter of when you are in an appropriate situation to give someone a compliment.

A compliment is like a mini gift, a cost-free way to spread joy during the holidays. There is something uplifting about a compliment. It makes people feel good, both the person giving and the person receiving the compliment. It's nice to be noticed for something. It's nice to know that someone can see and appreciate the effort you took with your appearance or your work, your idea or even your choice of a place to have lunch. We all know this, so why should we be stingy with compliments?

Giving a sincere compliment forces you to notice something positive. It must be sincere. That way it forces you to find the positives. I have never had a negative reaction to a genuine compliment. Handing out these free gifts can make two people smile at the same time. It also takes your mind off yourself and whatever you were worrying about.

62

TELEPHONE SOMEONE
YOU HAVEN'T SPOKEN TO ALL YEAR.

Sometimes Facebook postings like to show posters that explain friendship—like how really good friends can be apart for a long time without making contact and then pick up where they left off when they do get in touch. I have a few friends who fall into that category, and it's true that they are really good friends. The nice thing about these kinds of friends is that you don't have to apologize or make excuses for your lack of being in touch. You know they understand in the same way that you understand that they have been busily involved in their own lives as well. With the busyness of Christmas, it's hard to maintain even your regular contacts, but what a wonderful gift it would be for friends to hear each other's voices at this time. Familiar. Friendly. Like comfort food for the soul.

Several of my closest friends balance jobs, family and church work, and one winters in Jamaica, so we rarely get many chances to talk. Still, when we do, it is as if we had last spoken yesterday. It makes all our electronic communications via email and social networks seem about as personal as a bumper sticker—one way messages completely devoid of awareness of the state of the individual reading or receiving them. A telephone call can at least get some tonal information conveyed, but I would step up this recommendation to newer methods of communication now. The important thing is to do it. Years ago, the telephone company ads used the slogan "Reach out and touch someone." Now you can reach out and Skype, Facetime, Instagram, and Tweet someone. In other words, do whatever your skills and equipment will allow to take this concept even further—to make contact, and do that only if you absolutely can't manage to meet.

63

MEDITATE ON MIRACLES.

Is it possible to meditate on something? I thought meditation involved calming and clearing the mind and focusing on breath not thoughts in an effort to achieve some higher state of consciousness. I feel quite sure "meditate" was not really what I had in mind when I wrote this suggestion. Perhaps I meant "ponder miracles." It was probably something far more like, "Wow, this Christian birthday holiday is the start of a story that's full of miracles including the greatest miracle of all, but don't miracles happen all around us every day if you really think about it? Let's think about miracles."

That's pretty much my take on miracles. They happen every day. They may be inexplicable or even scientifically impossible and may involve some divine or supernatural intervention, something generally rather unlikely, but they are also to be seen everywhere in the everyday events of our lives. Every baby born is a miracle, even if the doctors think they understand the biology of it. Every flower that blooms is a miracle, regardless of the depth of our understanding of botany. A seed falls, or I put an ugly brown ball in the ground in fall and a beautiful bloom appears in spring. Every newly discovered cure is a miracle, and the people who work to develop them are miracle workers. Things that are really quite startling and seemingly impossible are happening all around us every day.

The story of the birth of Christ is the story of the greatest miracle of all, the one that rises above all others and persists beyond comprehension. The birth is the miracle Christmas, a gift of life, everlasting life—a miracle. Think about it.

64

APPRECIATE THE HUMOR IN EVERY SITUATION.

What is your worst story that seemed horrible at the time but in retrospect makes you laugh? "Remember the time when...?" The questions can be the basis for family game without losers, because sharing the stories creates a whole new round of laughter about shared experiences that were perceived as awful at the time.

"Remember the time you meant to send me an email complaining about your awful colleague and you accidentally sent it to him?" Horrifying at the time. Humiliating. Hard to survive or hope anyone will ever forget. Hysterical in retrospect. Those were the kinds of things I was thinking about twenty years ago. I thought it would be really great if we could see that potential for humor at the time of the incident instead of not until later. I was thinking of those awkward moments we all have.

Now, I think I must have been crazy to write this. Or, maybe there wasn't so much awful stuff going on twenty years ago in our pre-9/11, complacently secure lives. Maybe the embarrassing moments were the worst of it. Surely there is no humor in the really horrible things that have happened and continue to happen in our lives

But humor, if you'll forgive my saying so, is a funny thing. I know a young man who suffered a horrific accident. In one night, a strong, athletic, healthy, twenty-one-year-old became a quadriplegic. He clung to a thread of life while being airlifted to a trauma center for emergency surgery. When I was talking to the family about the long night they spent there, praying for his life and trying to support each other, one of them told me, "There were a lot of tears, and a lot of laughs." That surprised me at first, and then I got it. Aristotle described both tragic and comic theater as cleansing of emotions for the audience, and the stories we tell each other are nothing less than our own little personal dramas, the telling of which serves the same purpose as tragedy and comedy. I feel sure no one in that loving family laughed about the young man's accident, but I have no doubt that humor helped them through that night.

Try to find comedy in the face of tragedy, especially when your tragedy is nothing worse than a failed soufflé. Just think about how many people will relate to and laugh at your story, or at the picture you took of your collapsed soufflé when it's posted on social media.

65

REALIZE THAT THE DINNER WILL NOT BE READY ON TIME, NOR WILL THE GUESTS.

What is time anyway? It only really matters when you are running out of it. And I don't mean before dinner. Look it up. Apparently scholars actually debate what time is and haven't come up with a universally accepted definition. Who knew? And all the while I thought it was pretty clear, and the only problem was what the clock said when I wanted to talk to somebody on the other side of the globe.

The point here is what really matters in terms of enjoying your Christmas. I remember one holiday dinner when the unnaturally gigantic turkey wouldn't get done. The hostess was a good cook, and she meticulously followed cooking directions. But this big bird just defied the first law of thermodynamics. It simply would not achieve the edible internal temperature. What I remember most about that day, besides the uncooperative fowl, is that there was a whole lot of laughter shared while we entertained ourselves waiting for dinner and each time the oven was opened, the bird tested and the oven closed again. It wasn't a disaster. It wasn't a tragedy. It was the unexpected opportunity for the creation of shared memories.

And then there is the question of when the guests will arrive. I don't know if all of the etiquette guru's have agreed on whether or not one should be "fashionably late," but not too many people worry about those rules anymore anyway. People are late because a whole bunch of preventable or unavoidable things happen, and let's just leave it at that. Some are late, some are early, and anyone who ever hosts a dinner has to juggle the variables. Forget the juggling. You can't juggle things you can't control. Assume whatever. Keep it in perspective. It's not your last supper.

66

IN A CROWDED STORE, NOTICE SOMETHING NICE ABOUT EACH PERSON IN LINE.

Imagine this scenario. You had a busy and perhaps particularly challenging day at work. The press of business kept you from running out at lunch to pick up those things you wanted. You are in a hurry to get home, because you forgot to defrost dinner (pick up the kids/meet a colleague or whatever puts the time pressure on you), but one of your friends came back from lunch with the news that a certain big box store just received a new shipment of that impossible-to-find, electronic, score-of-the-year gift. You rush to the mall and find the only parking space available is practically in the next town, and you pull in even though it is so small you have to get out sideways and will likely suffer some bruises or door damage as a result. You hurry across the parking lot as fast as the icy surface and blowing wind will let you, and when you get to the store, you grab the very last one of the items left off the shelf. You are elated. You won. You rush to the front of the store only to find that there are at least twenty people in line by each beleaguered checkout clerk and the self checkout machines are all out of order.

Let's be honest here. Is this when our good charity or Merry Christmas spirit is likely to spring forth in abundance? Are we going to think kindly of the people in line ahead of us, each of whom has a piled-high cart, a tired, hungry and whining child and a fistful of questionable coupons or items without tags? I must admit that in several variations of this scenario, I found myself inclined to be just a tad critical of others, maybe even judgmental. Thoughts like "Why doesn't that person have their child home in time for dinner?" might have entered my mind. Or, "Does that person really need to buy all those things?" I have been guilty of this, and that is exactly why I came up with this challenging exercise—to exorcise that evil right out of myself before my head started spinning around unnaturally while I uttered curses in some lost language.

The goal is to notice something nice about each person in line. Try it in a supermarket line on a Friday night at some other time of the year (maybe all year) when the pressure isn't quite so high. The amazing thing is, it really works. First of all, if you are looking for something, and particularly for something that strikes you as "nice", you tend to let go of some of your tension and may actually find yourself smiling when you do succeed. You may even lose track of the fact that time is passing, so the line will seem to move faster. I know it sounds hokey, but before you knock it, try it. You still may not get home as quickly as you hoped, but you will be in a far better mood when you do.

67

RESIST THE URGE TO MAKE A GINGERBREAD HOUSE.

My gingerbread houses always looked more like the "before" in a television house renovation program than the "after." They always collapsed at the seams where the frosting didn't seem to work as mortar at all. I don't know why it should. Frosting and mortar have very little in common. And then there was the weight of the excessive amounts of candy that was piled on. We always started out with symmetrical and precisely geometric designs with alternating colors and mini-marshmallow accumulations of snow, but somewhere in the process we would get carried away and overdo things. The gingerbread part would be totally masked by what looked for all the world like there had been a natural disaster in the candy aisle and someone ought to call for cleanup.

These confections were never consumed, except for the sampling during the construction process. They would sit out on display for the entire holiday season, our proud accomplishment collecting dust and the stray pine needle or bit of glitter, as time passed. Extracting a piece of candy from the roof became as unappealing as it was impossible, as the frosting did eventually turn hard as mortar where it affixed the goodies to the cookie walls and roof. Eventually, in the cold light of January, the gingerbread house became an accusatory symbol of the excesses of the season, an embarrassment that carried a dollar and sentimental value that made it hard to discard. In retrospect, the whole of it was a very complicated business.

What did matter was that we had a great time doing it, that it became a tradition and that each year we seemed to forget the previous year's disaster and look forward with great anticipation to this annual event. It always involved a lot of laughter, mutual effort and togetherness. For these reasons, I think now that I will actually reverse my earlier suggestion and recommend making a gingerbread house, as long as you can overcome the complicated emotions involved. It will be necessary to give up the hope of perfection, to understand the value of failure in a joint effort, and to recognize the importance of the good time shared. I recommend saving the Halloween or Easter candy or whatever of it might be recycled to minimize the cost. Edibility is not an issue here. This can be, in the end, a grand adventure in creating memories.

68

KNOW THAT MATERIAL GIFTS ARE NOT THE MEASURE OF FRIENDSHIP, NOR CAN THEY CREATE LOVE.

I recently presented someone with a gift, and the look on that person's face made it clear that the gift was obviously not something he needed, wanted or thought was particularly special. My immediate reaction was to wonder if I could crawl under the rug and sink trough the floorboards. Never mind that he wasn't gracious enough or good enough at acting to spare my feelings.

But, what's wrong with that picture? What was I expecting from that offering? I was expecting the person to be or act happy, so I could feel good about having done something or given something that made him happy. That would make my happiness dependent on his happiness which in turn was dependent on my gift. That all seems rather complicated and insignificant in a good friendship, and of course it is.

The fact that my friend didn't act like that gift was something he really wanted didn't impact our friendship. It wouldn't be much of a friendship if it had. Although it was a bit of a surprise at the time, I'm happy to know that my friend is too honest to be phony.

Gifts are nothing more than tokens of friendship or love. They can neither create nor damage real friendships, nor can they create or destroy true love. It's the friendship or the love that is precious, not the gift. Share the experience of friendship. Share the love. Never mind the gift.

69

THINK ABOUT THE BEAUTY OF YOUR TREE BEFORE IT IS TRIMMED, AND MAKE SURE YOU HAVE A GOOD TREE STAND.

I imagine your happy family loves the annual get-the-tree-day, that is if you are one of those die-hard, must have a live tree families. Here's how I envision the scene: everyone gets up early excited to go. Then I see you all bundled up in plaid woolens and smiles (Polartec doesn't work in my scene). I see you frolicking in the snow, rosy-cheeked, finding the perfect tree, and riding back with it in the farmer's wagon while singing Christmas carols. Unless you live in the city, in which case I see you strolling by the tree stand that is festooned with lights that glimmer through the gently falling snow. The city scene ends there for me because I have no idea how city dwellers get their trees home (on top of a taxi?). Nor can I imagine such a charming scene for people who live in, say, Hawaii or South Carolina. We northerners have cornered the market on Christmas tree farm images.

I hate getting the tree, partly because I hate the cold, and partly because it rarely ever turns out to be such a jolly outing for me. I also hate the thought of severing the life of something so beautiful. I love the way trees look while still attached to their roots and growing out of the ground. I really think that anything we do to them is gilding the lily. You can't make it look better, you can only make it look like something else. I hope everyone thinks about how pretty the tree looks and then decides not to cut it. You could still have your picturesque outing, playing in the snow and all that. Then you could ride back in the wagon and talk to the other people who cut trees about being green-conscious and how they just killed something beautiful. Let me know how that works for you.

If your tree-harvesting experiences have been less than picture perfect, but you are determined to persist in the practice, the best thing I can suggest is to have good equipment; warm coats (Polartec is good), boots that don't leak, a sharp saw, plenty of rope, plenty of cash, a plan to get the thing home painlessly, and a really good tree stand, a great attitude and a lot of patience. Trust me, I speak from experience here. Maybe if I had those things, I would enjoy it more.

70

KNOW THAT GOOD FRIENDS
ARE BETTER THAN BIG PACKAGES.

Cliché alert! Who wouldn't have said, "I know that"? Geico insurance company ads on TV say that about the savings they offer, "Everybody knows that." This suggestion about packages and friends reminds me of that. I like to get gifts. We all like to get gifts (well, most of us do), and good gifts are better than, say, fruitcake. But no gift, no matter how big, is better than a good friend.

Think about it. What would be the best possible, biggest, most superlative thing you could receive as a gift (keyword "thing")? A big diamond? A new car? A villa in Tuscany? Of course any of those would be wonderful, and I'm standing by like Janis Joplin waiting to hear from Dialing for Dollars to see if anyone wants to gift me with any of those things. Would that make you my friend? It might at least suggest that you like me.

We have all kinds of friends. Accidental or casual friends are the people we befriend because they are there. They are there where we work, so we have lunch together or chat at the water cooler about last night's episode of whatever. They may be people at church with whom we are involved only slightly on short or long-term projects. They may be the parents of our children's friends with whom we sit through the infinitely long spring baseball or fall soccer seasons. Occasional friends are the ones we share a class with or a book club—the ones we encounter in neighborhood settings. But good friends are the ones that we all are lucky to have wherever they are. They are the ones who will be there when you need them, the ones who don't judge you, who love you, who know when you do or don't need them and so on. You know who they are, and there is nothing better.

Go ahead and buy gift cards for all the accidental, casual or occasional friends you want to acknowledge but don't know all that well. That's a much better choice than trying to figure out what to get them. Give your good friends a box of their favorite candy or that special soap you know they love but probably won't buy for themselves. Or best of all, give them some of your time. It is the best thing we can give each other.

71

HAVE PLENTY OF PACKAGE WRAPPING, VIDEO AND AUDIO TAPE ON HAND.

Another one bites the dust of obsolescence. Some of us still have plenty of those old audio and video tapes around, but the machines that operate them are breaking down, and no one wants to bother to fix them. They linger to the bitter end in garage sales until the Salvation Army truck or the dumpster appears. Those tapes are no longer what you want to stock up on, but have become something you want to get rid of. This suggestion now seems rather like a time capsule, or an item you find in your closet that appears surprisingly quaint and outdated.

Technologies do become obsolete quickly, and new ones are developed every year, but most often progress is a good thing. I love the fact that electronic storage devices are requiring less and less space now, because I don't have to worry about dusting the albums before I pull up the pictures on my hand-held device to share with someone. I love that I can instantly share those pictures with people in other time zones and on other continents.

We can be glad that we no longer need those video and audio tapes, but we do still need to make sure we have enough sticky tape to wrap packages. Settling in to piles of presents, surrounded by rolls of paper, holding a good scissor and listening to Christmas music sounds delightful. But that pleasure and progress can come to an abrupt halt when that last bit of tape splits off on your finger and you realize there is no more.

72

PRACTICE HUGGING.

When I decided this year to embark on an exploration of all the suggestions I had made in the book I wrote twenty years ago, I did not have a specific plan about how to get started, pace myself or stay focused enough to finish. So, I typed the list of the suggestions and I looked at it every morning to see which one inspired me to write some expanded text. As it turns out, this one, "Practice Hugging," was the last one to be considered, perhaps because it is a touchy subject. Please forgive the pun, because the fact is, it is a touchy subject.

I, for one, believe in hugs as a kind of enhanced handshake; that is, I am not just greeting you, but letting you know that I care or am willing to care for or about you. I'm OK hugging or getting hugs from just about anybody in just about any situation. To me, it's a kind of human-to-human huddle that probably dates back to the age of "Maybe if we stand this close together, the wooly mammoth will think we are bigger than we are and go away," or, "Dang, that ice keeps coming, but if we stand this close, we can share our body heat."

So much for my speculations on the origins of hugs. I could go on through the ages, but I think that's enough of my banter. The fact is, some people are not really open to sharing a hug. Perhaps they think it is unprofessional or perhaps they want to restrict it to something sexualized. These are the people who really need to practice hugging—not just practice, but actually make it a practice.

If you are one of them and feeling a bit unsure about how this is done without those negative connotations, you can go to the internet where there are lots of links to instructions. Caution: some of these might scare rather than encourage you. Instead of that, I would recommend you start with a friend, an aunt, or a sibling and just open your arms the next time you greet them.

Practice, if you need to, and get at it right away, not only because of all the love you are missing, but because of all your love you are not sharing with others. If you are one of those wonderful, warm and friendly people who hugs just about everybody everywhere, God bless you. You are a professional hugger. Keep practicing anyway.

73

IF SOMEONE HAS EVERYTHING, MAKE A CHARITABLE DONATION IN THEIR NAME, BUT DON'T GIVE OUT THEIR ADDRESS.

The key here is to let your gift recipients know personally that you have supported a cause they believe in. Say it in a card. It's a wonderful idea, a wonderful gift, and the people who have everything will probably appreciate that you didn't buy them something they don't need. Some charities, although not all, will send the person a thank-you for the donation but may also include him or her on the list for future solicitations. The last thing you want to do to your friends is open their mailbox to future solicitations. The donation site or solicitation should make clear whether they do this or not. If it's not clear, don't provide your friend's contact information. They can choose to continue donating to that cause if they want to, and they might want to do it anonymously.

If you can't think of an appropriate charity, or don't have the contact information for one you have in mind, turn to the miracle of this modern age, the internet. Here are some good places to start looking.

American Institute of Philanthropy's "Charity Watch"
http://www.charitywatch.org/toprated.html

The Better Business Bureau's "Charity Reviews, Ratings and Guides" http://www.bbb.org/charity-reviews/national/

Charitable Organizations' 990's can be viewed at The National Center for Charitable Statistics http://nccs.urban.org/

A charitable gift is probably the only really perfect gift—the gift that truly embodies the spirit of Christmas—the all-around best gift even for those people who don't have everything.

74

THINK ABOUT YOUR THREE BEST ACCOMPLISHMENTS THIS YEAR.

If you think about this and come up with a list that includes a great stock trade, a promotion or a big commission, you are on the wrong track. Think again. Did you stop for that person who held a hand-lettered sign asking for money, dry a tear, or carry someone's groceries? Did you go the "extra mile" to help out someone who really needed your help doing something even though it was really not a good time for you to do it? Did you offer an anonymous donation to a worthy cause or volunteer your time and talents to a worthy project that could well use your expertise? These are the things I'm talking about. Think about it. What have you done this year that really touches your heart? That makes you feel all warm and cozy inside-that seems consistent with everything you were taught as a child.

I believe that God's Grace shines down on all of us whether we try to pile up points through good deeds or not. Still, knowing that you made the right choices, that you did the right thing, is a good thought to reflect on. These choices, made throughout the year, are the continuation of the spirit of Christmas. Thinking of them during the holiday season can help you maintain your balance. No purchased gift has the same value as giving of yourself—your time, your talents, your compassion, or just your willingness to listen. Those are your best accomplishments. Thinking about them during the holiday season will help you maintain a perspective on what really matters.

75

RELAX AND ENJOY.
YOU'VE DONE EVERYTHING YOU CAN.

Perhaps this should have been the last suggestion in the book. Or, maybe the first. It rather sums up the whole of all the other suggestions. Christmas abounds with beautiful potential, but the best of it isn't reflected in perfectly polished silver. The beauty comes in the form of fumbled hugs, crooked smiles from kids who just lost a tooth, and spending time (relaxed time) with friends and family. Whether you have spent the weeks leading up to it, or even a good part of the year or maybe only the last hours at the mall getting ready, when Christmas gets here, enjoy it.

Don't fret about what you could have done, should have done, might have done, or what Mr/s Jones did next door. You did what you did. Maybe that will be an awe-inspiring challenge to others. Maybe the local paper will write about your decorations or charitable works. Maybe nobody will even see or know what you did. What matters is that you relax and enjoy the beauty of the season, the sincere wishes for peace on earth, the glittering lights, however perfect or imperfect, the warm smiles, the familiar scents and the love people share.

I think it is simply grand that people make an effort to make others happy, especially at Christmastime. Whatever you have done, is what you could do. It is enough. Relax and enjoy. Repeat after me:

It is enough.

Relax.

Enjoy.

76

SING CHRISTMAS MUSIC EVERY DAY.

I mean sing, not listen to. Not hum. Sing. Really sing. My dad had a beautiful tenor voice, and he used to get up every morning and go outside in his bathrobe and sing. Really loud. It might have been anything from church hymns to opera or the song he sang so frequently to my mother that I still have all the lyrics memorized: "Let Me Call You Sweetheart." The tune still gets me misty eyed. It never occurred to me, or probably to him, to wonder what the neighbors might think. Of course, at Christmas, he sang carols.

There is something about Christmas music that makes us all want to sing at most any time of day. Is it the familiar tunes that remind us of the good times, or maybe the happy or spiritual lyrics that touch our hearts? It's probably something that doesn't warrant a great deal of examination. It's part of the joy, something we share because we have all heard these songs and know these songs, and most of us do want to hear them again year after year.

Sing your heart out, even if your voice isn't so great. Psalm 100 says,

> Make a joyful noise unto the LORD, all ye lands.
> Serve the LORD with gladness: come before his presence with singing.

Because I was not blessed with a beautiful voice like my dad, the key word for me here is "noise." Clearly this particular Psalm is telling me to go ahead and sing anyway, and I do. I sing Christmas music every day and everywhere during Christmas, and I recommend the practice to everyone.

77

TAKE NOTES FOR NEXT YEAR.

Keep a Christmas ledger for the soul, not a gift list or a card list. What worked this year? What didn't? Someone once told me that the Mayans' understanding of good and evil was centered around a concept of "what nourishes is good and what doesn't nourish is not good." I have no idea if that has any archeological or contemporary validity, but I really like the idea.

I'd like to apply that measuring stick to Christmas activities, if not to an even wider range of daily activities and practices. What is it that we do that nourishes? What doesn't? Clearly a Christmas dinner provides nourishment, but if done or consumed in excess, it does not. And all that other stuff that we do at Christmas, is it nourishing us, our souls, or those of the people around us?

I have seen Christmas card registers that provided space to enter names and addresses like a regular address book but then had a series of columns and years with little boxes to tick off to indicate whether a card was sent and/or received from each of those people in those years. I can't imagine anybody does anything like that anymore, at least not without the help of an Excel spreadsheet, nor can I see the value in that. I'm thinking about a place where you could actually take notes for next year. A diary perhaps? Or, little sticky notes that you could pack up with your Christmas decorations. Maybe I should make a page for notes at the back of this book. Yes, I think that is exactly what I will do. Take notes in the back of this book. In fact, there is a good deal of white space on all of these pages, so have at them. Make notes wherever.

78

WEAR FLANNEL.

I was almost tempted to change this to "wear fleece" now, because of its superior warmth, weight and washability, but it's just not the same as flannel. There is something so wonderful about flannel—a kind of mystique that grows from the associations that go with it and link us to its Scottish tartan origins.

Flannel carries the recollection of soft plaid winter shirts and the love of the people who wore them. It reminds me of being warm in the outdoors, linings in windbreaker jackets and even in winter weight jeans. It was the fabric of receiving blankets in which we swaddled our babies and the changing pads we put under them for freshening up. Sunday schools had flannel boards with flannel cut outs that could be pressed on to tell stories. Flannel was winter pajamas all buttoned up and cozy and smelling like the fresh air.

My mother used to hang our flannel clothes outside and let them freeze stiff as boards on the line before bringing them in and draping them over radiators to dry or to heat up to toasty levels before being worn again. How could that not warm your heart as well as your body?

If you are a fashionista and not the type to actually wear flannel, you are still in luck. Flannel sheets are widely available in all sizes, colors and prints and go on sale in spring. "Wear flannel" is a feel-good suggestion, extended now to include sheets as well as clothes. Feel the warmth. Feel the history. Feel the love.

79

ASK FOR HELP IN THE KITCHEN.

You might have figured out by now that almost all (maybe all) of the suggestions in this book are based on some personal experience of mine. I'm guilty. I have overextended myself at holiday time.

"No, no," I say to my family and guests, "you go sit down and visit. Enjoy yourselves. I can do this," as I juggle the pots and pans or chop the onions, both of which cause streams of tears to flow down my face. What's wrong with me? Or, what's wrong with you, if you do this?

Help! Help!

Wouldn't your friends or family respond if they hard that cry somewhere, even if it was a stranger calling out? Of course they would. Every day we hear stories of people being heroes, jumping onto subway tracks or running into burning buildings or wherever to help others. Wouldn't you respond the same way, especially if the cry was coming from someone you loved? No brainer. Right?

So why do I (or you) stand in the kitchen, plugging away at the chores there, straining my ears to catch a word or two of the entertaining conversation going on out of earshot? People can talk in the kitchen. People like to be heroes, especially when it requires nothing more dangerous than drying pots.

The kitchen at Christmastime when a holiday meal is being prepared or cleaned up is a great place to let people be heroes. Ask for help, even if you don't really want it. Just have somebody arrange the veggie tray alphabetically or something. It makes them feel useful and important. That's a good thing, and then you (I) won't be alone. I'm going to try it. If you do too, let me know what happens.

80

FOOD IS GOOD.
TOO MUCH FOOD IS NOT GOOD.

Really? You know you are going to regret it. Every gym and sports store in the country knows the same thing; that you are going to be coming in looking for active wear and a treadmill within a week after Christmas. They were probably stuffing their storerooms with these goods while you were still Christmas shopping. Gyms will all advertise special prices for membership. The staff of the very same magazines that featured five-million-calorie holiday treats on their covers in December were wrapping up their "best-diet-ever" issue before they went home for the holidays. And, you've got to know that all those "shed pounds fast" promises on their covers are either not going to work, or you are not going to do what they require. It would seem that everybody knows these things, so who are we fooling when we make New Year's resolutions that we might not have even needed if we had been a little more prudent during the holidays.

I'll admit to being the first to belly up to the table for a good feast. There is a lot to be said for that. The Christmas dinner table is one of the most likely times to find families together. What an opportunity to enjoy each others' company along with some delicious food. Food ought to be part of a celebration, not the point of the celebration.

I don't believe that one Christmas dinner is going to do anybody much damage, not even one delicious, excessive, over-the-top Christmas dinner. The problem is that the starting gun for the season of gluttony goes off at Thanksgiving, and it goes off with a very large bang. That Thursday leaves a good four to five weeks when hosts and hostesses try to outdo themselves or their neighbors with elaborate spreads of exceptional foods; hors d'oeuvres, appetizers, many courses and absurdly tempting desserts. And drinks. What about eggnog? Beginning with Thanksgiving, it's all downhill. It's the parties and the lunches and the liquor and the snacks and the cookies and the candies and everything else that we indulge in, "because it's Christmas." Mid-January, when you're despairing about your weight, you might just scream if someone suggested a nice, rich high-caloric eggnog with whipped cream on top. So why did you drink it three weeks ago when it sounded oh, so good, and after all, it's Christmas? Why do we turn Christ's birthday holiday into a month-long Baccanalia?

Maybe 20 years from now, when the tide of obesity has finally turned, this section of my book will need to be deleted. I hope so. Meanwhile, I hope I can remember to try to maintain some sort of perspective and not spend whole evenings hovering over the pots of Swedish meatballs, the trays of butter cookies and the punchbowls full of eggnog.

HAVE A VERY MERRY CHRISTMAS!

Please do. Don't make yourself crazy. Don't make others crazy. Be merry. Think about what it means when you say "Merry Christmas," and mean it. There is a true meaning of Christmas. It is connected to love and giving. It is about God's love for us and our love of God and for each other. I haven't meant to trample the trappings we've learned to expect as symbols of this spirit. I only hope that I have inspired a reader or two to think about what they do and feel at this time of year and to consider it carefully. What does it really take to love and to give? I think the answer can be pretty simple. I really, sincerely do wish you a perfectly Merry Christmas.

NOTES

NOTES

ABOUT THE AUTHOR

Helen Isolde Thomas, MA, is a free-lance writer, author and Grants Writer *Emerita* from the State University of New York at Geneseo. She is also a former middle school English teacher, Administrator of the Strong Memorial Hospital Pain Clinic, and Area Personnel Director for Service Systems Corporation. She has lived in both England and the United States and traveled widely elsewhere. She currently lives with her three cats and one very large goldfish in New York's Finger Lakes Region.

In addition to her first book, *How to Have a Perfect Christmas: Practical and Inspirational Advice to Simplify Your Holiday Season* (Dutton, 1996), she has written for an eclectic collection of print and electronic venues including; newsletters too numerous to mention, *Life in The Finger Lakes* magazine, *Green Prints: The Weeder's Digest, livinglutheran.com, The Well-Being Journal, Lutheran Forum, and* in the books, *Reviving Ophelia,* and *An Encyclopedia of Broadway and Culture,* as well as on several editorial pages.

Made in the USA
Middletown, DE
10 November 2015